Reboot

Reboot

A Business Novel About Money, Finance, and Life

Gary Smith and Margaret Smith

Reboot: A Business Novel About Money, Finance, and Life

Copyright © Business Expert Press, LLC, 2025

Cover design by Margaret Smith and Gary Smith

Interior design by Exeter Premedia Services Private Ltd., Chennai, India

All rights reserved. No part of this publication may be reproduced, stored in a retrieval system, or transmitted in any form or by any means—electronic, mechanical, photocopy, recording, or any other except for brief quotations, not to exceed 400 words, without the prior permission of the publisher.

First published in 2025 by
Business Expert Press, LLC
222 East 46th Street, New York, NY 10017
www.businessexpertpress.com

ISBN-13: 978-1-63742-624-1 (paperback)
ISBN-13: 978-1-63742-625-8 (e-book)

Business Expert Press Finance and Financial Management Collection

First edition: 2025

10 9 8 7 6 5 4 3 2 1

Description

A novel about personal finance—and life.

Reboot tells the story of Lisa, who is recently divorced and confronted with many of the potentially intimidating financial decisions we all must make.

She learns about:

- Credit cards
- Car loans
- Home buying
- Social security
- Retirement living
- and more

as she takes control of her finances and her life from a place of curiosity and self-respect. One reviewer wrote: "*Drama blends with practical money smarts. Join this captivating journey to financial stability.*"

Contents

Testimonials ix

Chapter 1	A Shattered Dream	1
Chapter 2	A Forty for Two Twenties	7
Chapter 3	It's Not Whether You Win or Lose	11
Chapter 4	Falling Off a Cliff	15
Chapter 5	Pulling Out of the Nosedive	17
Chapter 6	Where to Begin?	21
Chapter 7	Of Course, I Can Afford It	27
Chapter 8	The Time Value of Money	31
Chapter 9	Sperling's Rule	39
Chapter 10	Brother Michael	45
Chapter 11	Moon Cakes at Midnight	49
Chapter 12	Home for Rent, Home for Rent	55
Chapter 13	Your Home Is an Investment	59
Chapter 14	Home Sweet Home	63
Chapter 15	This Old House	67
Chapter 16	Good Day Sunshine	73
Chapter 17	Social Security	79
Chapter 18	Other Retirement Accounts	91
Chapter 19	Life Insurance	97
Chapter 20	Annuity Snake Oil	101
Chapter 21	Peaceful Place	107
Chapter 22	Fake Intelligence	113
Chapter 23	Turning a Page	117
Chapter 24	The Crossover	121
Chapter 25	Sadly Ungrateful	127
Chapter 26	Control the Small Stuff	133
Chapter 27	Control the Big Stuff	143
Chapter 28	The Greater Fool Theory	153
Chapter 29	A Benevolent Casino	159
Chapter 30	Stocks in the Long Run	165

Chapter 31 Mellowing Michael 175
Chapter 32 A Life Reboot 179
Chapter 33 Summing Up 183

About the Authors 187
Index 189

Testimonials

"*I am so enjoying your book. I think it's brilliant to put this information in the form of a novel. It reminds me of one of my favorite books,* The Way of the Peaceful Warrior. *In it, the master is teaching the student through conversations and as the reader, you anticipate each meeting for the new insights, just as I am doing with this book. This book has walked my husband and me through the common pitfalls that we and so many of our peers have made, and given us practical and smart systems for finding financial strength, growing our wealth, and most importantly giving us peace of mind.*"—**Natalie K.**

"*Inspiring! This quick, entertaining read by Margaret and Gary Smith provides a different lens to view the common financial issues most of us face throughout adulthood. Readers will walk away armed to tackle pervasive obstacles to wealth building such as debt, fear, and dubious financial recommendations.*"—**Theresa H.**

"*Lisa so eloquently asks all the embarrassing questions I've wanted to ask for years but didn't have the knowledge or courage to ask. I found myself taking notes and mirroring the story in my own life. What a gift the Smiths have given us in sharing their knowledge and expertise, wrapped up in a story.*"—**Robin O.**

"*Drama blends with practical money smarts in* Reboot. *Join this captivating journey to financial stability. I will definitely recommend or require* Reboot *as reading material in my personal finance courses.*"—**Mitch Mokhtari, Professor of Personal Finance, University of Maryland, College Park**

CHAPTER 1

A Shattered Dream

"That son of a bitch!"

Lisa had been a good daughter, a good wife, and a good mother—well, not perfect, but certainly better than just okay. She shook her head and said it again, even louder, "That son of a bitch!"

How did her dream become her nightmare?

****

Lisa's parents were born in Taiwan. They met in college and were married two weeks after graduation. Six months later, they traveled halfway across the world to a Los Angeles suburb called Diamond Bar so that their children could live the American Dream. Lisa was born a year after they arrived and her brother, Michael, was born a year later.

Diamond Bar is a planned community built on the site of the Diamond Bar Ranch, a cattle, pig, and horse ranch that used a "diamond-over-a-bar" branding iron. It's a quiet residential community that has terrific schools and is 60 percent Asian-American. Just what Lisa's parents had hoped to find in America—friendly faces in a clean city that had better weather and more opportunities than Taiwan.

They arrived in America with almost no money and not speaking a word of English. But they both spoke Fortran and Cobol and soon had jobs working for a software company that had been started by a cousin who had come to the United States a decade earlier. Houses were cheap and, with help from friends and relatives, Lisa's parents were soon able to make the down payment on a three-bedroom, two-bath tract home. Their monthly paychecks were (barely) enough to cover the mortgage payments, but they had a house they could call home in a place they wanted to call home.

They were thrifty—which is a polite way of saying cheap. The kids mostly wore unisex clothes so that Michael could wear things that Lisa outgrew. They only went to movies once a year, during the Christmas holidays, and were not allowed to buy popcorn: "We're not going to pay $5 for something I can make at home for 50 cents." Instead, they smuggled snacks into the theater by hiding them in their jacket pockets. Yes, they lived in Southern California and wore jackets to the movie theater, no matter what the temperature was outside: "The air conditioning will give you a cold." It wasn't easy sneaking in popcorn in plastic bags and drinks in sports bottles, but the jackets made it work.

Speaking of air conditioning, they never turned on the heater or air conditioning in their house. Temperatures in Southern California are moderate, but there are days over 100° ("You think this is bad? In Taiwan, it is hot *and* humid!") and nights below 40° ("Put on another sweater").

No one in the family ever went to a barbershop for a haircut: "We're not paying $10 for something I can do at home for free." Plus, short hair is easier to wash and brush. Lisa and Michael didn't know enough to complain.

They seldom went to restaurants: "We're not paying $40 for something I can cook at home for $4." When they did go to a restaurant for a special treat, like the celebration of a birthday or academic award, they never ordered drinks or desserts: "Water without ice is fine and American desserts are too tián (sugary)."

The parents scrimped on things they could live without so that they could give their children things that were important—Chinese school, violin lessons, tennis training, and anything else that would help Lisa and Michael become successful Americans.

Still, the family thriftiness was sometimes embarrassing. When family gatherings were held at their house, guests were given napkins made from paper towels torn into four pieces, and served water in paper cups with the guests' names written on them. At the end of those rare restaurant meals, mom would put any uneaten food into leftover boxes and swoop packets of salt, ketchup, and such into her purse, along with unused paper napkins that could be torn into fourths at home. Any water remaining in glasses was poured into the sports bottle that mom carried everywhere.

Neither of Lisa's parents ever became fluent in English, but they were determined that their children would be "real Americans"—that's why they gave them popular American names and dressed them in popular (but cheap) American clothes. Lisa and Michael both spoke English without a trace of an accent and, for better or worse, adopted many American habits, including (eventually) ignoring their parents' incessant yapping.

Lisa was particularly high-spirited, but she shared her parents' ambitions and carried out their grand plan. Throughout elementary, intermediate, and (especially) high school, when Lisa wasn't at Chinese school, or taking violin or tennis lessons, she studied for her classes and for the SAT tests that would determine her future. She was a school Asian, not a cool Asian.

Diamond Bar High School was full of students like Lisa, but she was determined to be valedictorian and she was. Her perfect SAT scores sealed the deal, and she was accepted by both Yale and Harvard. As with many Chinese families, the choice was obvious: Lisa went to Harvard. Years later, Lisa realized the deep irony—Asian families are obsessed with Harvard, but Harvard does not return the affection.

No matter, Lisa made it through Harvard's snooty admission process and was off to Massachusetts—snow and snobbery be damned. She studied almost as much at Harvard as she had in high school and graduated *summa cum laude* with a degree in psychology.

She was recruited by a global software company to be part of a sales team based in Irvine, California—which delighted her parents. They did not want to leave their family and friends in Southern California in order to be near Lisa, and Irvine is firmly in Southern California.

Irvine is a planned community in Orange County. The Irvine Ranch, 100,000 acres, plus-or-minus, stretched from the Cleveland National Forest down to the Pacific Ocean. The ranch was used mainly for cattle and sheep in its early days, then came barley and other field crops, and finally citrus. Orange County got its name from the fact that its weather is near-perfect for growing oranges, and several thousand citrus trees were planted on the Irvine Ranch. They're almost all gone now.

After nearly a hundred years of ranching and farming, the Irvine Company realized that its land would be worth a lot more if it was used for homes and businesses to accommodate Southern California's explosive growth. In 1961, nearly 1,000 acres were sold to the University of California for $1.00 for a new campus, the University of California, Irvine (UCI), and another 500 acres were sold to the University at a discounted price in 1964. UCI was soon up and running, along with its irreverent mascot, the Anteater, a name chosen by UCI students. (Among the other options on the ballot were Bison, Centaurs, Roadrunners, Toros, and "none of these"—which came in second.)

The Irvine Company then began developing the surrounding area. The part of the ranch surrounding UCI became the City of Irvine; other slices of the ranch became parts of other cities, including Laguna Beach, Newport Beach, Tustin, and Anaheim.

Irvine is a suburban community with pockets of homes and businesses linked by freeways and wide streets with 50-mph speed limits. There are lots of parks and athletic fields, community swimming pools, hiking and biking trails, and great schools. Some people think it is sterile; others think it is paradise.

Irvine is only 30 miles from Diamond Bar but, with California traffic, that could be more than an hour of bumper-to-bumper frustration. So, Lisa's parents moved to Irvine, which, like Diamond Bar, has a vibrant Chinese-American community. By now, they were able to afford a newly built house, which many Chinese-Americans covet because, then, they don't have to worry as much about finding trustworthy workers to fix things that need fixing.

Lisa's parents could now see Lisa regularly and were hoping to become grandparents soon.

Grandparenting would have to wait. Number 1: Lisa didn't have a boyfriend, let alone a husband. Number 2: Lisa was determined to use the same work ethic that got her into Harvard and through Harvard *summa cum laude* to sprint up the corporate ladder.

Lisa had seen firsthand at Harvard how winners play the game of life. They dress differently. They talk differently. They even walk differently. They have a casual confidence that borders on casual arrogance. A Japanese-American boy she met at Harvard said that when he visits Japan, the locals can tell immediately that he is American. Lisa felt the same way about the kids at Harvard who came from successful families and were on their own fast tracks to successful lives. She could tell just by looking that they were different.

Lisa followed their lead. Her parents were modest. Lisa was confident. Her parents were frugal. Lisa spent money, lots of money. The Silicon Valley computer jockeys in t-shirts and sandals or sneakers had not yet taken over the world. Haircuts and clothing still mattered, so Lisa got expensive haircuts and wore expensive clothes.

Lisa was in sales where it pays to make a memorable impression. She had met more than enough lawyers, realtors, and Wall Streeters to know that they are all essentially salespeople who spend money creating an image of prosperity. "Dress for success" is a cliché but, like many clichés, there is a lot of truth in it. People are more easily persuaded to buy this or do that by people who appear to be successful.

Lisa's self-assurance was only partly a facade. Hey, she had graduated *summa cum laude* from Harvard, which was a lot more than most of her customers could say. Even when the computer geeks ascended, Lisa's work ethic and self-assurance closed deals. Her base salary was 250K and, with commissions, she was making more than a million a year.

Lisa was not only very good at making money but also very good at spending money—a nice home in Irvine, a vacation house in the mountains, four expensive cars, and a giant walk-in closet full of overpriced clothes. She did yoga and jogging because these were efficient ways to maintain her looks. She played tennis and golf so that she could network with actual or potential customers.

Along the way, she met Erik, a tall, blonde, and handsome Swede. Not-so-subtle flirting, whirlwind dating, and soon they were married with children. Erik was, in theory, a self-employed consultant but, in reality, he was not that interested in putting in the time needed to make serious money. Why should he bust his butt when Lisa was busting hers?

Erik did almost all the cooking, cleaning, and child care and told his friends and strangers that he was a retired consultant. He relished the fact that other women praised him for being enlightened. He appreciated the fact that household chores were not at all like the business world where success is measured in dollars and cents—and Erik had not been successful.

At age 42, Lisa was living the dream in a Southern California McMansion, making more than a million dollars a year, with a 16-year-old son, Noah, an 18-year-old daughter, Anna, and a tall, blonde, and handsome Swedish husband.

Their child-raising years were winding down, and they would soon have more time and money to spend on themselves and with each other.

It was the calm before the storm.

CHAPTER 2

A Forty for Two Twenties

How had Lisa not seen it coming? Lisa knew that she was a handful, but she thought that when Erik called her "feisty," he was complimenting her. She made good money, let Erik buy anything he wanted, and laughed at his dumb jokes. The sex was good enough. She gave him everything he wanted and sometimes enjoyed it herself. What could he possibly complain about?

She knew that Erik looked at porn on the Internet. She knew that he stared too long at what he laughingly called "large-breasted chickadees." She saw him flirt with young mothers at soccer games and assumed that this wasn't the only time and place that he was flirty. Heck, she flirted, too, when it suited her. It was fun and often helped close deals, but she never took it to the next level.

Erik did.

She once overheard him joking with his brainless buddies, "Yeah, when she gets to be 40, trade her for two 20s." Yuk Yuk.

Lisa wondered why so much male humor is at the expense of women, but, then, she knew many women who liked joking about their husbands, boyfriends, and assorted male losers:

Why don't men show their true feelings? Because they don't have any.
What do you call a man who lost all of his intelligence? A widower.

Erik wasn't a widower, but he certainly lost the brains in their marriage when they split up.

One of Lisa's friends said, "What was he thinking?" Lisa immediately answered, "Clearly, he wasn't thinking," and added, "Not that he ever did." After she found out that Erik had strayed, she wondered how many times he had cheated on her. Not that it mattered. Once is too many.

They all agreed that men mainly think with their penises and that life would be a lot easier if men could keep their pants zipped. Lisa said,

I think it's in their genes. They are just hard-wired to roam. The hell with them. I will never again unbutton my blouse for a man.

Erik had gotten caught when some bimbo showed up at their house while Erik was "doing errands." She was young and perky and did not seem to be standing on the front porch because she was selling cosmetics or campaigning for mayor.

Hi, I'm Tammy and I'm looking for Erik.
And I'm Lisa, Erik's wife. What, exactly, do you want?
I know who you are, Lisa, and, yes, I know Erik's still married. My guess is that you don't know who I am.

That gave Lisa something to think about. "Still married?" Was he expecting to soon be unmarried? She was curious but increasingly furious. Instead of pulling hair and scratching faces, they used words as weapons:

Who, again, are you? And why are you standing on my front porch harassing me?
I'm Tammy, Erik's current girlfriend and future wife. Your husband and this front porch will soon be mine.

Tammy turned and left, wiggling her firm butt as she strutted off the porch and down the brick walkway.

Lisa slammed the front door and headed upstairs to the master bedroom. "Where the hell is Erik? Is he off riding another mare in his stable?" Not that it mattered at this point. Lisa opened a window and began throwing all of Erik's clothes on the front lawn. The sky was sunny, as it often is in Southern California, but Lisa would have prayed for rain if she were religious.

Step 2 was to get a locksmith to change the door locks ASAP. Step 3 was a yard sale Saturday for the rest of Erik's crap—one dollar for all you can carry. Step 4 was to find a good lawyer.

CHAPTER 3

It's Not Whether You Win or Lose

Erik got himself a female lawyer, Catherine Steinhaus, thinking that this would show the judge that he wasn't a chauvinist pig. Lisa had to admit that Catherine put on quite a show. She was as pleasant as could be outside the courtroom and a pit bull inside. Catherine had an audience of one and it wasn't the judge; it was Erik. She was the embodiment of an oh-so-true lawyer joke:

It isn't whether you win or lose, but whether your client is happy to pay the bill.

Erik was happy to pay the bill, especially after his pit bull lawyer told him that Lisa would have to pay Erik's legal bills because she had a job and Erik didn't. NumNuts Erik didn't think it through. California is a no-fault-divorce 50–50 state, so half of every dollar going to their lawyers came out of Erik's pocket.

During a break in the proceedings, Lisa saw one trick Catherine used to inflate her bills. She took out a list and made brief check-in phone calls with maybe a dozen clients:

Hi [first name]. It's Catherine, just calling to see how you are doing and if anything has come up....
Good. I'll let you know if anything happens on my end.

The calls averaged maybe a minute apiece, but Catherine billed in 15-minute intervals. At $800 an hour, she charged each client $200 for a minute of her time. In all, she spent maybe 15 minutes on a dozen pointless phone calls and racked up $2,400 in legal fees. Her $800/hour rate ballooned to $9600 an hour.

If Erik's lawyer was all sizzle, Lisa's lawyer, Howard Green, was all steak. It is hard to imagine a more boring man, but he knew the law better than Catherine (and maybe better than the judge!). While Catherine tried to keep the meter running, Howard tried mightily to keep things moving forward. He wasn't interested in running up legal bills. His refreshing attitude was, "If you take the legal costs into account, is it worth haggling over this?" The truth is that most items weren't worth the legal cost of being mentioned—let alone arguing about.

Still, with Catherine protesting everything that she could protest and unleashing a tsunami of dubious claims, the case lasted nearly two years and the bills added up to roughly $600,000 by the end of this nightmare, two-thirds charged by her, one-third by Howard. As expected, the judge had Erik and Lisa each pay $300,000.

There was no child support because Noah and Anna were now over 18 but Lisa was ordered to pay Erik $35,000 a month in spousal support and, because they had been married more than 10 years, the spousal support would continue until Erik either remarried or died. Erik wasn't planning on remarrying and, at his age, wasn't likely to die soon—though Lisa did have some vivid dreams about creatively painful ways of making that happen.

Lisa had been betrayed by Erik and, WTF, she had to give him $35,000 every month so that he could maintain his swinging lifestyle and never have to lower himself to take a job. Lisa was beyond incensed:

> *What a bunch of bull. He goofs off while we're married and, then, he cheats on me and gets rewarded for his sins by being allowed to keep goofing off for the rest of his lazy life.*

Erik got the family house (so that the kids wouldn't have to move out), but at least bimbo Tammy didn't get the house or Erik. Turned out he did have other girlfriends and wanted more, and it was far easier to find sexually generous women now that there wasn't a wife lurking around.

Most women are looking for a commitment and are understandably skeptical about promises made by a guy who is cheating on his wife. Once the wife is out of the picture and the scoundrel blames the ex-wife for the breakup, his hunt is a lot easier. Of course, Erik moved on after every conquest, adding to his mental tally of ex-girlfriends.

Their kids didn't seem surprised by the divorce. They had spent most of their time before the divorce with Erik, and they were old enough and smart enough to know that he wasn't happy.

Truth be told, Lisa felt a bit (not a lot) of sympathy for Erik after the divorce was finalized. He had a college degree, was personable, and was basically a good guy. He was surely disappointed that the career he had trained for didn't work out. It had to be embarrassing for him to hang around parks and soccer fields with nannies and grandparents. He was a good father and an okay husband who didn't feel appreciated because Lisa didn't say thank-you enough (okay, not at all). Maybe it is different in Sweden, but Lisa's parents never thanked each other, and Lisa didn't think that she needed to thank Erik for anything he did—or that he needed to thank her for everything she did.

Erik wasn't the first or last person to have a mid-life crisis.

CHAPTER 4

Falling Off a Cliff

The discovery of Erik's infidelity was a gut punch for Lisa. The divorce was a slow-motion, seemingly never-ending pummeling. But these were hardly her only struggles.

She had always been the best. She had been high school valedictorian. She had been the best psychology major at Harvard. She assumed that she would be the best salesperson at her firm, but she wasn't. Her blood pressure and cholesterol were far too high and her mood was far too depressed. She was stuck in a cycle of triple espressos to stay awake in the daytime and triple shots of cognac to fall asleep at night—which made her tired and grumpy during the day and restless at night.

She was burned out.

After one presentation she gave at work, her boss told her,

Lisa, you were talking 200 words a minute with gusts up to 500. It was like watching a light bulb get very bright just before it goes dark.

Lisa was desperate. She got a nose job, boob job, and butt job. She spent more money than ever, trying to convince herself that her hard work was worth it.

Instead, she felt the opposite. She barely knew her children and they barely knew her. It was painful for her to remember leaving for work before the kids were up and coming home after they were asleep. It was heartbreaking to remember their disappointment when she missed their soccer games and school plays. It was embarrassing to remember how she was always checking her phone while they were trying to talk to her. Was it worth it? Did she really need so much money? Did she really need two houses and four cars?

The sour cherry on top was that Lisa had let Erik handle all the family finances because she was so busy with her job. She made the money and he paid the bills. Once she was on her own, she quickly realized how clueless she was. The divorce revealed how much they had spent each month (a lot) and how little they had saved (hardly anything).

She also discovered that Erik had gone on a revenge-spending binge at the end of their marriage—partly because of frustration and anger at Lisa and partly as retail therapy for himself. Some people pig out on ice cream when they are sad, others take trips to Cancún. Erik chose Cancún—along with an elite credit card that let him hang out in VIP airport lounges, upgrade to first-class on planes, and rent fancy cars. He stopped making dinner for himself and the children and, instead, binged on DoorDash, Uber Eats, and other delivery services. He bought expensive massages that (mostly) were real massages. He bought expensive jewelry for his many girlfriends.

Lisa wondered who had chosen the smarter path.

CHAPTER 5

Pulling Out of the Nosedive

Lisa reacted differently than Erik to the wreckage of her marriage. She didn't do any revenge-spending or indulge in retail therapy. Her parents' thriftiness had sunk deep hooks. She could justify spending to advance her career, but she couldn't bring herself to spend for the sake of spending. Instead, she set out to reclaim her health—to become the feisty, indestructible Energizer Bunny she had been when she was young.

Lisa joined a club and started playing tennis regularly, not to close deals but to rebuild her body and let off steam. She loved smacking the ball hard as she made a loud grunt (what some call "shrieking"). She had seen a television show where some high school kids let off steam by going to a junkyard and smashing things with a sledgehammer. Lisa felt the same way when she walloped a tennis ball.

She also took up boxing at her club. Not that she wanted to be in an actual boxing match. She just found that boxing training was great for pretty much all parts of her body and gave her a tremendous hormonal high. Punching a bag or a person was a better workout and even more fun than thumping tennis balls.

It was at one of these boxing workouts that she met Jasmine. They were both women and about the same age and size, so they got paired up for some friendly sparring. It was great! Jasmine was as feisty as Lisa and also just as stubborn. Neither would back down until the instructor intervened,

Enough is enough, girls. Save some for our next class.

They were both dripping sweat and deliriously happy. They touched gloves firmly and sat on a bench rehydrating.

Jasmine was also divorced. (Is there something about men not being able to deal with feisty women?) Her parents had immigrated from Iran and settled in Irvine, along with many other Persians. She majored in economics at UCI (had to stay close to home) and then headed off to Wharton Business School to get an MBA with a major in finance. Wharton is one of the best finance schools in the world and, unlike most MBA programs, doesn't make students work for a few years before applying. It's also on the East Coast and Jasmine thought it would be good for her to get away from her parents for a few years.

As Lisa listened, she kept thinking déjà vu, déjà vu. Lisa was Chinese and Jasmine was Persian but, other than that, they were like twinsies. Jasmine was having the same thoughts as Lisa recounted her life story.

There were, of course, differences; in fact, some big differences. For one, Lisa was clueless about managing money and Jasmine was an expert. Also, Jasmine had deliberately avoided the corporate rat race, turning down Wall Street offers so that she could open her own financial-consulting business and be her own boss. She hadn't taken a job she hated in order to buy things she didn't need. She hadn't burned out like Lisa.

As Jasmine worked with clients, she realized that Wharton had stuffed her head with plenty of financial theories that she was eager to apply to the real world. However, humans don't always behave the way finance professors assume they do. Money problems are often not money problems at all but, instead, reflections of a client's personality.

If someone doesn't pay their bills on time, for example, it usually isn't because they don't understand the consequences but, rather, because they have trouble being organized. Bills might be stuffed, unopened, and forgotten in a pile of other papers, while late-payment penalties accumulate. The solution is not to teach these messy people how financial penalties are calculated but to help them become better organized.

Jasmine also discovered that many people practice *mental accounting* by thinking of their money as separated into compartments. For example, tax refunds are used to pay for vacations, so the bigger the refund, the better the vacation. Another form of mental accounting is the idea that impulse purchases can be justified and paid for by money saved on other purchases:

Charlie: We can buy a 48-inch television because I returned the couch I bought yesterday.
Cameron: I wish you had bought and returned two couches. Then we could buy a 65-inch TV.

Once Jasmine recognized the importance of human personalities, she studied the Enneagram and other coaching systems and the wisdom she learned became an integral part of her advising practice. Her financial-consulting business morphed into a coaching business. She wouldn't tell a client, "You're an Enneagram Type 3" (an achiever), but she would take the personality type into account when she worked with the client. (BTW: Jasmine was already pretty certain that Lisa was a Type 3.)

Lisa was fascinated:

Sign me up. I need help. I need it badly and I need it soon.

Jasmine had not been trying to make a sales pitch, and she was normally hesitant to give advice to family and friends. It's like selling your old car to a friend and having the car break down soon after.

Still, Lisa seemed like she needed help with her money and her life and Jasmine wanted to help:

Sure, I'm happy to. How about Tuesday morning at 10:00? Here's the address.

Lisa knocked on Jasmine's door Tuesday at 9:55, excited and hopeful.

CHAPTER 6

Where to Begin?

Jasmine's office was a large room in an unexpectedly modest home. The location was certainly spectacular. Looking out the floor-to-ceiling windows, Lisa could see large vegetable and flower gardens to the east and the Pacific Ocean to the west. She could hear wind chimes and birds and see butterflies and rabbits.

The home was a one-story ranch house, at most 1,500 square feet, with a bedroom, an office, two bathrooms, and an open floor plan that made the floor-to-ceiling windows the focus of the house. The floors were oak planks and the furniture was sparse.

Jasmine poured two glasses of sparkling water, which they took into the area she used as her office. There was a large oak schoolteacher desk, a hundred years old from the look of it, but Jasmine didn't hide behind the desk. They sat in facing leather chairs, which could have been Restoration Hardware reproductions but were probably originals, sipping their water and smiling at each other.

Lisa had questions, lots of questions:

I've been working my tail off for a long time, being incredibly successful and making darn good money. Erik and I were living like millionaires, but we're not millionaires. After paying our lawyers, we're broke! Why don't I have any savings? Why did I lose my family? Why am I so unhappy?

Jasmine replied calmly:

I think it helps to make a distinction between being rich and being wealthy.

I say that someone is rich when they have lots of money and material possessions. I use the word "wealthy" to describe someone who is living well, someone who feels peaceful, someone who is healthy and happy with their life. Money does matter, of course, but more money does not always make you happier; sometimes, it tempts you to do things that make you sadder.

The difference between rich and wealthy is like the difference between inner peace and outer looks.

Jasmine then told Lisa about a life-changing moment that happened when she was at Wharton. Near the end of one class, a student asked a famous professor whether it was better to take a job in management consulting or investment banking. Investment bankers can make a lot more money, but they also generally work a lot more hours under much more pressure.

The professor smiled mysteriously and, after a moment of letting all the students ponder the question, said calmly,

I firmly believe in the old adage, "If you love your job, you will never work a day in your life."

The best job is one where you wake up in the morning looking forward to going to work, the job you would do even if you weren't being paid to do it.

If you take a brutal job just for the money, no matter how much money, you will eventually quit and you will regret and resent the years that you suffered.

The professor held up his hand to silence any questions. He wanted the students to think about what he had just said. Then, he gave the punchline:

I could have made 10 times as much money working on Wall Street, but I love the job I have. I love sharing what I know with bright students like you. I love my colleagues. I love having the freedom to do research and write papers and books on whatever it is I want to do research and write about. I love not being on someone else's schedule. There are classes and committee meetings but, otherwise, I do whatever I want to do when I want to do it. I love my job and I have never worked a day in my life.

He then said a few words about Dave Swensen, who had been his classmate in Yale's Economics PhD program. After getting his PhD in 1979, Swensen was hired by Salomon Brothers and, three years later, moved to Lehman Brothers. Three years after that, at age 31, he took an 80 percent pay cut and returned to Yale to manage their endowment.

Swensen later explained that he had accepted the job and pay cut because, "There are a lot of important things in life you don't measure in dollars and cents." For Swensen, some of these things were teaching college students, playing poker with Nobel laureate James Tobin, being on a summer softball team with Yale's president, Rick Levin, watching Yale hockey games, and coaching his children's baseball and soccer teams.

His management of Yale's endowment was spectacular, and he could have gone back to Wall Street and made a fortune, but he loved his life at Yale and stayed there until his premature death from kidney cancer in 2021.

The professor began tearing up and concluded simply:

That's all for today. I hope you will always remember what I just said. If you do, that will be, by far, the most important thing you learn in this class.

Jasmine teared up a little too as she remembered this life-changing story.

Lisa saw the damp eyes and asked Jasmine if she loved her job, even though the answer was surely yes. Jasmine said,

Yes, I do. I love helping people, especially people I care about. Plus, and I haven't told you this yet, I also like writing books about money and about the Enneagram. One of my little tricks when I'm writing is to stop in the middle of a thought; in fact, in the middle of a sentence. Then—while I am biking, showering, going to the bathroom, whatever—I think about what I want to say next and what words I want to use to say it. The next morning, I can hardly wait to get out of bed because I am so excited about writing down these words and thoughts.

My job and my life are completely intertwined and I love them both.

Then Jasmine steered the conversation back to Lisa:

Lisa, I don't know you well yet, but I will. From what you told me after our boxing class last week, I feel that you are stuck in a job where you tell lies in order to get people to pay more than they should for things they don't really need.

Lisa looked very sad as she nodded "yes," so Jasmine went on:

I want you to spend some time thinking about what you would love to be doing with your life. Something you could be truly passionate about. Don't be impulsive. Really think about it. Don't take two hours or two days. Take two months. Longer if you need to.

You were a psychology major at Harvard, maybe something related to that. You're a terrific salesperson. Maybe you would be fulfilled selling something you believe in. If you're stuck, with no promising ideas, talk to other people and see if what they're doing seems interesting.

We're talking here about what we hope will be a long-term commitment so try to be as sure as you can be sure that this is it.

Lisa nodded again and Jasmine concluded,

While you are thinking about a life you could love, we'll work on your financials. I don't know why you saved so little when you earned so much, but I am confident that we can figure it out. I want you to gather all the financial statements that were used in your divorce case and any updates since then. Drop these off here before the weekend and, next Tuesday, we'll start.

Lisa nodded a third time, then gave Jasmine a long hug and left—hopeful that this was the beginning of a better life.

CHAPTER 7

Of Course, I Can Afford It

Lisa dropped the financial statements off at Jasmine's house on Wednesday (yep, three days early) and knocked on Jasmine's door at 9:55 Tuesday morning (yep, five minutes early). She was eager to learn the answer to the big mystery of how she could have made so much money and have so little to show for it. What in the heck had Erik done?

After a welcome hug, they each took a glass of sparkling water into Jasmine's office and settled into those comfy leather chairs. Jasmine got right to it:

Wow! We have a lot to talk about. I am going to try to keep it in bite-size chunks, so we will talk about one main thing every week or two, depending on our schedules.

Lisa was a bit taken aback. She wanted to know all the gory details about how she ended up in this financial quicksand and how to climb out of it, but Jasmine made it sound pretty intimidating. Did they really need several weeks to get through it all?

Jasmine sensed Lisa's anxiety, so she smiled and reassured her:

Don't worry. None of it is very complicated. There is just a lot to talk about. We will walk through it, one step at a time, and, you will understand everything. Trust me. And when we're done, I'll give you a handy set of rules to remember.

Lisa looked relieved, so Jasmine went on:

Today, I think we should talk about credit cards.

I've looked over the papers you gave me and I can see that there have been many questionable decisions, but one overwhelming problem is credit cards.

Let me ask you, "Do you know how credit card companies make money?"

Lisa honestly had no idea. She might have guessed that people pay something like a membership fee every year, but she vaguely remembered Erik bragging that they had no-annual-fee credit cards (until he went on his revenge-spending spree). Jasmine explained,

Some cards have annual fees. Merchants also pay a small charge on every transaction, but most of their profits come from the interest the credit card companies charge on unpaid balances.

If you pay off every penny of your balance every month, there are no interest charges. But once you slip up and don't pay the full amount you owe, the unpaid balance is considered a loan and they charge you interest on that loan. After that, every transaction you make immediately adds to the loan balance and to the interest you pay.

Lisa cheerfully wondered, "So they charge you interest, how bad could that be?"

Jasmine made an "oops" face and answered,

Bad, really bad.

Right now, credit card interest rates average around 24 percent and they calculate the interest you owe every single day and add that interest to the amount you owe. This means they charge you interest today on your unpaid balance and then charge you interest tomorrow on that balance and on the interest they charged you the day before. By charging you interest on interest every day, the effective interest rate is boosted from 24 to 27 percent.

Outside of loan sharking, it is hard to think of a higher interest rate on borrowed money. In fact, there is an episode of the Sopranos TV show, where Tony Soprano says that his father taught him that

loan sharking and credit cards are based on the same principle: You hook people on borrowed money and then bleed them dry by charging them interest on their unpaid interest.

Since Erik had handled all the bills and other finances, Lisa had no idea how much they owed on their many credit cards or how much interest they had been paying. She was not happy when Jasmine told her that they were paying 27 percent interest on tens of thousands of dollars of credit card debt. Even worse, the interest paid on a home mortgage is often tax deductible, but credit card interest is not.

Jasmine was gentle:

One problem with credit cards is that there is a temptation to think, "Of course I can afford it; I'll just put it on my credit card." For people who give in to this temptation, the cost of that impulsive purchase, including the 27 percent interest, is much higher than the price tag on the purchase.

For people who can resist that temptation, credit cards are a great convenience. You don't have to carry cash and you don't have to monitor your checking account balance constantly to make sure that your checks don't bounce. You use your credit cards whenever you can and pay your credit card bills on time every month.

However, and it's a big however, credit cards are outrageously expensive if you don't pay the balance due every month.

Lisa clearly understood, but Jasmine said it anyway:

The only way to beat the system is don't borrow from loan sharks or credit card companies.

This means that the first step to financial fitness is to pay off your credit card balances. We need to get money out of your bank accounts, sell stocks, whatever, so that we can pay off your credit cards. Paying off a credit card balance on which you are being charged 27 percent interest is like making an investment that gives you a guaranteed 27 percent rate of return.

> *I'm going to give you some more investment advice in a few weeks, but I'm telling you right now that no other investment is guaranteed to be so profitable.*
>
> *Let's do it!*

Jasmine and Lisa then went through the blizzard of credit card bills and bank statements, scrounging for money they could use to chop down Lisa's credit card balances. Fortunately, she was able to pay them all off without touching her retirement accounts or taking out a second mortgage on her house—or doing something even more drastic, like selling her house. The credit card quicksand had not yet swallowed her.

When they were done, they both beamed. This had been a great session!

Lisa hadn't yet figured out what she wanted to do with her life so Jasmine said,

> *No worries. Choosing a job is like choosing a spouse. Getting it right is more important than getting it done quickly.*
>
> *In the meantime, we have plenty to talk about. Let's meet again in two weeks and we'll dive into something that sounds boring, but is actually the key to almost all financial decisions—the time value of money.*

Lisa had no idea what Jasmine was talking about, but she hoped that it would be as eye-opening as their deep dive into credit cards.

CHAPTER 8

The Time Value of Money

Lisa was early as usual for their next meeting and eager to see what she would learn, though she doubted it would be as valuable as escaping the credit card quicksand. She was wrong. It was even more valuable.

After they settled in, Jasmine said,

This isn't going to be a no-brainer like paying off your credit cards, but we are going to talk about one of the most important ideas in finance—something that will save you many tens of thousands of dollars over your lifetime.

Lisa's eyes widened as Jasmine started a dialogue:

Jasmine: *Would you rather be paid $1,000 today or 10 years from now?*
Lisa: *Duh, now, because I could spend it now without having to wait years.*
Jasmine: *What if you weren't allowed to spend it for 10 years?*
Lisa: *Then, I guess it wouldn't matter. Either way I would have $1,000 to spend 10 years from now.*
Jasmine: *The thing is, if you had $1,000 now, you could invest it and have a lot more than $1,000 10 years from now.*
Lisa: *Oops! I forgot about that. How much more?*
Jasmine: *Well, that depends on the rate of return you earn. I calculated some examples last night. If you invest $1,000 in bonds paying 5 percent, you will have $1,629 in 10 years. If you earn a 10 percent annual return (roughly the historical long-term average return on stocks) you will have $2,594.*

Jasmine let Lisa think about that for a few moments and then gave the takeaway:

The reason that money today is worth more than money in the future is that money today can be invested. This difference between money today and money in the future is called the "time value of money."

Lisa agreed:

It seems so obvious. I don't know why I didn't think of it that way.

Jasmine smiled, happy that Lisa understood, and she reassured her:

You're hardly alone Lisa! Many smart people completely ignore the time value of money. It can be a huge mistake.

For example, there is a federal law called the Truth in Lending Act that governs most consumer loans, including home mortgages. One of its rules is that lenders must show borrowers the total payments they will make over the life of the loan, including the amount borrowed and the interest charges.

I call that "the total payments error" because it completely ignores the time value of money.

Lisa looked confused, so they took a break to make smoothies. Then, Jasmine said,

I want to show you some nerd numbers I came up with last night. Is that okay?

Lisa nodded "yes" and Jasmine quickly showed her a computer printout before Lisa had a chance to change her mind:

Suppose you are going to buy a new car for $50,000 to replace what has become a clunker and your employer offers to lend you $40,000 for anywhere from three to eight years at a 3 percent interest rate.

The three-year loan has monthly payments of $1163.25 and total payments of $41,877.00. The eight-year loan has monthly payments of $464.18 and total payments of $45,041.28. So it is tempting to think that the three-year loan is the better option because it has lower total payments:

Loan	Total Payment
3-year loan at 3%	(36 months)($1,163.25/month) = $41,877.00
8-year loan at 3%	(96 months)($469.18/month) = $45,041.28

Lisa looked at the numbers that Jasmine had printed out and quickly agreed that the total payments were lower for the three-year loan.

Then Jasmine reminded her that it's a mistake to compare the payments without taking into account when they are made:

Remember the time value of money. A dollar three years from now is worth more than a dollar eight years from now—so it is a total payments error to compare the payments without taking into account when the payments are made.

Lisa frowned:

Okay, okay! You got me again. But if I shouldn't compare the total payments, how do I decide which loan is better?

Jasmine replied,

There is a mathematical calculation called the "present value," which takes into account the time value of money and always give the correct answer. Unfortunately, the calculations are a bit complicated—so, I'm going to save them for when we really need them.

For now, we can use a simple rule of thumb. Let's talk it through.

Lisa: *Okay, I like rules of thumb.*

Jasmine: *What if you borrow $1,000 for one year at a 5 percent loan rate and invest that $1,000 for one year, earning a 10 percent return. Would you make money or lose money?*

Lisa: *Is this a trick question? It seems pretty obvious that you make money.*

Jasmine: *What if you only earned a 2 percent return?*

Lisa: *You lose money?*

Jasmine: *Exactly. So it is profitable to borrow money if you can earn a rate of return that is higher than the loan rate.*

Lisa: *Yep.*

Jasmine: *So, in our car loan example, borrowing money at 3 percent is a good idea if you can earn more than a 3 percent return on your investments.*

Lisa: *Makes sense.*

Jasmine: *Exactly. So if you can borrow at 3 percent and earn more than 3 percent, you generally want to borrow as much as you can for as long as you can. Take the eight-year loan.*

Lisa: *That makes sense, too.*

Jasmine: *That's your rule of thumb!*

Lisa: *That was easy.*

Jasmine: *Most financial decisions are just common sense but there are pitfalls (like the total payments error) that need to be avoided.*

Lisa smiled. She loved the rule of thumb because it is simple and it makes sense. Jasmine noticed the smile and then showed Lisa two tables of calculations she had made the night before.

Here's the brute force way to compare these two loans. Remember that the monthly payments are $1,163.25 for the three-year loan and $464.18 for the eight-year loan.

Lisa nodded, though the tables looked like a big blur of numbers. Jasmine pushed on:

> Suppose you have made your $10,000 down payment on the car and have a bank account with $40,000 earning 3 percent. You could take $40,000 out of the bank and pay cash for the car, leaving you with nothing in your bank account.
>
> Or you could choose the three-year loan and leave $40,000 in your bank account. Every month, you take $1,163 out of your account to make the monthly car payment. Believe it or not, the first table shows that, at the end of three years, your bank balance will be zero—the same as if you had paid cash. Borrowing at 3 percent in order to earn 3 percent on your bank balance is a nothingburger.
>
> Alternatively, you could choose the eight-year loan and take $464.18 out of your bank account every month to pay off the loan. Numbers don't lie. The second table shows that, at the end of eight years, your bank balance will be zero. Again, borrowing at 3 percent to invest at 3 percent is a nothingburger.
>
> These two tables show that our rule of thumb is right. It doesn't matter whether you borrow for three years or eight years if you borrow at 3 percent to earn 3 percent. Either way, it's a wash.

Lisa gushed, "Wow! I like the rule of thumb better than the tables." Jasmine laughed and continued,

> There's more. I also did two tables where the bank account is earning 4 percent, but I'm not going to show them to you until you answer two questions.

Lisa: *Try me.*
Jasmine: *If you take one of the 3 percent loans and the bank account is earning 4 percent, do you think the bank balance at the end will be positive, negative, or zero?*
Lisa: *Well, it was zero if you earn 3 percent, so it should be positive if you earn 4 percent.*
Jasmine: *Correct! And, for the grand prize, which loan will have the higher balance at the end of eight years?*

Lisa: *Well, our rule of thumb tells me that borrowing at 3 percent to invest at 4 percent is profitable, so doing that for eight years must be better than doing it for three years. I choose the eight-year loan.*
Jasmine: *A+. I knew you were a terrific student.*

Jasmine showed her two tables with the bank account paying 4 percent. One table shows that the three-year loan is paid off after 36 months and there is still $676.23 in the bank account, which can continue to grow for the next five years. After eight years, the bank balance is $825.67. The second table shows that the eightyear loan is paid off after eight years with a final bank balance of $2,076.36.

Jasmine said,

These tables are super complicated. I only showed them to you to convince you beyond any doubt that our rule of thumb is correct. There are four takeaways. First, borrowing at 3 percent to invest at 3 percent is a wash. Second, borrowing at 3 percent to invest at 4 percent is profitable. Third, borrowing at 3 percent to invest at 4 percent is more profitable the longer it goes on.

Fourth, It is a lot easier to use the rule of thumb than to construct tables!

Lisa was very pleased that the numbers confirmed her intuition. Jasmine was pleased, too, because Lisa now knew the rule of thumb and was convinced that it worked.

It was a great, meaty session where Lisa had learned two of the most important principles in finance: (1) the time value of money and (2) when it can be profitable to borrow money.

The second lesson was especially provocative. Lisa had always thought that borrowing money was a sign of weakness: "If you can't pay cash, then you can't afford it." The reality is much more nuanced. Maxing out your credit cards to buy junk you don't need *is* foolish. But when you can borrow money at a low interest rate to buy something that you do need, it is actually better to borrow money than to pay cash.

THE TIME VALUE OF MONEY   37

That lesson was about to be put into practice, and it kept Lisa from making a costly mistake.

Using money in the bank earning 3 percent to pay off a three-year 3 percent car loan

Month	Bank Balance	Earned Interest	Car Payment	Net
1	40,000.00	100.00	1163.25	-1,063.25
2	38,936.75	97.34	1163.25	-1,065.91
3	37,870.85	94.68	1163.25	-1,068.57
⋮				
34	3472.37	8.68	1163.25	-1,154.57
35	2317.80	5.79	1163.25	-1,157.45
36	1160.35	2.90	1163.25	-1,160.35
37	0.00			

Using money in the bank earning 3 percent to pay off an eight-year 3 percent car loan

Month	Bank Balance	Earned Interest	Car Payment	Net
1	40,000.00	100.00	469.18	-369.18
2	39,630.82	99.08	469.18	-370.11
3	39,260.71	98.15	469.18	-371.03
⋮				
94	1400.54	3.50	469.18	-465.68
95	934.86	2.34	469.18	-466.85
96	468.01	1.17	469.18	-468.01
97	0.00			

Using money in the bank earning 4 percent to pay off a three-year 3 percent car loan

Month	Bank Balance	Earned Interest	Car Payment	Net
1	40,000.00	133.33	1163.25	-1,029.92
2	38,970.08	129.90	1163.25	-1,033.35
3	37,936.74	126.46	1163.25	-1,036.79

(Continued)

(Continued)

Using money in the bank earning 4 percent to pay off a three-year 3 percent car loan					
Month	Bank Balance	Earned Interest	Car Payment	Net
⋮				
34	4136.13	13.79	1163.25	-1,149.46
35	2986.66	9.96	1163.25	-1,153.29
36	1833.37	6.11	1163.25	-1,157.14
37	676.23	2.25	0.00	2.25
38	678.48	2.26	0.00	2.26
⋮				
94	817.47	2.72	0.00	2.72
95	820.20	2.73	0.00	2.73
96	822.93	2.74	0.00	2.74
97	825.67			

Using money in the bank earning 4 percent to pay off an 8-year 3 percent car loan					
Month	Bank Balance	Earned Interest	Car Payment	Net
1	40,000.00	133.33	469.18	-335.85
2	39,664.15	132.21	469.18	-336.97
3	39,327.18	131.09	469.18	-338.09
⋮				
94	3453.95	11.51	469.18	-457.67
95	2996.28	9.99	469.18	-459.20
96	2537.09	8.46	469.18	-460.73
97	2076.36			

CHAPTER 9

Sperling's Rule

Wouldn't you know it. Lisa was actually planning to buy a new car and, armed with her new rule of thumb, went car shopping. She found the car she wanted and negotiated a good price, but then the sales guy said that she should finance the car with a 12 percent loan. Lisa remembered the rule of thumb and doubted she was going to earn more than 12 percent, so she declined as politely as she could (though she was secretly annoyed that this smooth talker was trying to take advantage of her—perhaps because she was female and Asian).

Then, the guy showed her a newspaper clipping from the *Los Angeles Times*—not as great a newspaper as the *London Times* or *New York Times*, but still reputable. The *LA Times* columnist had interviewed Frank Sperling, a vice president at Security Pacific National Bank, about whether people should pay cash for a car or get a car loan. Sperling told the *Times* columnist that car buyers who get car loans can invest the cash they were planning to spend on the car and may make enough money to pay the interest on the loan and make a profit, too. Lisa recognized that type of reasoning from her last meeting with Jasmine, but then the newspaper column took an unexpected turn.

What rate of return did the car buyer need to earn on the invested cash to make the loan profitable? Sperling said that,

> *If you can earn an interest rate equivalent to half the interest rate on your loan, you'll come out ahead.*

The *Times* columnist called this Sperling's Rule.

When Lisa finished reading the clipping, the car sales guy put his hand on her shoulder, gave her a big toothy smile, and said, "See, all you have to do is earn a 6 percent return to make a 12 percent loan profitable!"

Lisa trusted Jasmine a lot more than the sales guy, but she couldn't figure out why Sperling's Rule was so different from Jasmine's rule of thumb. She told the sales guy she would think about it.

As soon as she was out the front door of the car dealership, Lisa telephoned Jasmine from the parking lot and was happy when she answered and even happier when Jasmine said,

> *OMG! Don't sign anything. Sperling's Rule is a scam. Either pay cash or walk away. I'll explain everything at our next meeting.*

Lisa walked away. She wasn't comfortable doing business with a scammer.

At their next meeting, Jasmine got right to the point:

> *I don't know if Mr. Sperling is uninformed or unscrupulous, but he's wrong. Either way, I wouldn't trust a car dealer who tried to pull this trick on me.*

Lisa beamed and said,

> *Yeah, I walked away because I no longer trusted him. So, what's the scam here?*

Jasmine explained:

> *The trick is that car loans (like most loans) are amortized, which means that the monthly payments not only cover the interest but also pay off some of the loan so that when the final payment is made, the loan is fully paid off. This mean that you are only borrowing the full amount, say $40,000, for the first month. The remaining balance that you are borrowing goes down every month. By the end, you are borrowing almost nothing. On average, you are borrowing about $20,000 and paying interest on about $20,000. So, Sperling is comparing the interest you pay on $20,000 with the return you earn on $40,000—which is why the loan rate can be almost twice the rate you earn on your investments and still seem profitable.*

Lisa nodded, but Jasmine wasn't sure that Lisa understood. Jasmine had anticipated this and knew that she would have to show Lisa some numbers, which is why she had prepared another nerd-table the night before:

I made a table like the ones I showed you last week. Sperling's Rule implies that if you borrow $40,000 at 12 percent and invest $40,000 at 7 percent, you come out ahead. Let's see what really happens if you follow this advice.

You have $40,000 in a bank account earning 7 percent and you could use this money to pay cash for the car. Instead, you take out a $40,000 five-year car loan and leave your $40,000 in the bank, using the bank balance to make the monthly payments. I calculated how much money you would have in your bank account after five years.

Lisa nodded,

Fair enough. Show me your table.

Jasmine showed her the table on the next page. The first month's interest on the bank account would be $233.33, not nearly enough to make the $889.78 car payment. Lisa would have to take $656.44 out of her bank account in order to make her car payment, which means that she would earn a 7 percent return on only $39,343.56 in the second month. And so it would go. Lisa would earn less and less interest each month on a shrinking bank account.

The table shows that Lisa would run out of money well before five years were up. At the end of five years, she would be about $7,000 in the hole.

Jasmine said, "See, Sperling's Rule is wrong and my rule of thumb is right: you lose money borrowing at 12 percent to invest at 7 percent."

Jasmine said that some people—not Lisa—have no choice because they don't have enough cash on hand. They may need a car to get to work and recognize that buying a car is cheaper than renting one every

Using money in the bank earning 7% to pay off a five-year 12 percent car loan					
Month	Bank Balance	Earned Interest	Car Payment	Net
1	40,000.00	233.33	889.78	−656.44
2	39,343.56	229.50	889.78	−660.27
3	38,683.28	225.65	889.78	−664.13
⋮				
53	256.28	1.49	889.78	−888.28
54	−632.00	−3.69	889.78	−893.46
55	−1,525.46	−8.90	889.78	−898.68
56	−2,424.14	−14.14	889.78	−903.92
57	−3,328.06	−19.41	889.78	−909.19
58	−4,237.25	−24.72	889.78	−914.50
59	−5,151.75	−30.05	889.78	−919.83
60	−6,071.58	−35.42	889.78	−925.20
61	−6,996.77			

workday; they may be convinced that buying a clothes washer and dryer is a lot better than frequent trips to a laundromat; or they may want to go to college to get a better job. In each case, if they can't pay cash, they are pretty much forced to either borrow or do without.

For people like Lisa who can pay cash, the question is whether it is better to pay cash or to get a loan and invest the cash.

Lisa sat quietly thinking things through and then made a very smart observation:

For some people, avoiding loans and paying cash may be a clunky way of controlling impulse spending. As they say, money can sometimes burn a hole in your pocket. When people get an unexpected bonus at work or win a cash prize, they may feel compelled to spend the money. In the same way, people who could pay cash to buy a car but get a loan instead may be inclined to spend the "extra" cash that they had planned spending on the car. Paying cash takes that money off the table so that they won't spend it on foolish frivolities that they don't really need.

Jasmine said,

That's a great point! I know that you and Erik had trouble controlling your spending and we are going to work on that. On the other hand, borrowing money to invest money can really build wealth. For example, borrowing money to buy a house can be fantastically profitable—a lot better than renting all your life or waiting several years or decades until you can pay cash for a house.

So, I am going to encourage you to borrow money when you can earn a rate of return that is higher than the loan rate, but I am also going to warn you not to borrow money to buy things you don't really need.

Lisa responded immediately:

I'm convinced. I do have a question, though. Housing prices in most places only go up a few percent a year, maybe 3 to 5 percent. How's that a great investment?

Jasmine answered,

In due course...

Due course arrived sooner than either of them expected.

CHAPTER 10

Brother Michael

Lisa and her brother, Michael, had never been particularly close. It was more like they had coexisted when they were kids. There were the usual sibling affection and rivalries, but Lisa and Michael were just, well, different people on separate paths. For one thing, Lisa was a lot more focused on getting the grades and test scores she needed to get into Harvard. Michael didn't even try.

Lisa was also a tomboy, while Michael was unusually small and not much interested in throwing, catching, kicking, or hitting balls. When he had to play team sports at school, he was always the last kid picked. It's not much comfort when you are Mr. Irrelevant (the nickname given to the last person taken in the National Football League draft) but the reality is that, as Bruce Springsteen sings, the glory days pass by quickly for most school jocks and they end up in dead-end jobs, working hard hours and living with disappointed wives while the geeks and nerds end up being successful businesspeople (think Mark Zuckerberg) or running the country (think Henry Kissinger).

Yes, it's a silly stereotype—the high school quarterback marries the head cheerleader and they live unhappily ever after—but there is a lot of truth in most stereotypes.

Michael didn't go to Harvard. He didn't go to college at all. Throughout high school, he spent more time watching television than doing homework. Irvine was growing rapidly, and Michael wanted to be part of the Irvine real estate boom. He didn't watch television out of boredom, but to prep himself to become a successful realtor.

He studied several compelling TV men, including trustworthy news anchors Tom Brokaw and Peter Jennings. He also practiced imitating the quiet charm of Johnny Carson and Alan Alda. His favorites were James Garner and Michael J. Fox. Garner was a rascal who starred in two great television series, *Maverick* and *The Rockford Files*, where he played a basically honest guy with an infectious smile who could sell ice to Eskimos, as they say. To Michael, that sounded like the key to being a successful realtor.

Even better was Michael J. Fox, who shared the same name and was short and baby-faced just like him. On his big hit, *Family Ties*, Fox has a tomboy sister and he wants to be rich. Sound familiar?

After high school, Michael got his realtor's license, joined an Irvine realty company, and soon had his own firm. Real estate is a tricky business because, for most people, buying a home is the biggest purchase they will ever make and they worry about making the biggest mistake of their lives. Buyers want someone they trust to tell them which home they should buy and what price they should pay. Sellers want someone they trust to tell them that they are getting a good price.

Michael is that someone—a disarming smile, an innocent baby face, and the reassuring voice of a news anchor. Michael is what's known as a "closer." When he senses that a buyer or seller is close to saying *yes*, he gives the final reassuring nudge. If a few well-chosen words aren't enough, he will put up some of his own money to bring the deal to the finish line. On a million-dollar home (and most homes in Orange County are now worth much more than that), Michael's commission is at least $20,000 and he is happy to put up a few thousand dollars of his own money to close any gap that exists between buyer and seller.

Michael also has lots of pocket listings, homes for sale that only he knows about because he has persuaded the sellers that he has a long list of buyers and can close the deal quickly and hassle-free at good price. If he represents both the buyer and the seller, he gets double commissions, at least $40,000 on a $1 million home and at least $200,000 on a $10 million home.

Michael's commissions are totally negotiable and he does his best James Garner impersonation to reach a commission arrangement that both he and the customer are happy with. Michael lives by the same philosophy as do many lawyers—it's not whether he gets the best outcome for his clients, but whether they are happy to pay his commission.

Michael likes spending and loathes saving. Expensive cars, clothes, and jewelry. He lives alone in a five-bedroom, seven-bath, 5,000-square-foot oceanfront property in Laguna Beach. He doesn't have a wife or kids, but he has more short-term girlfriends than any man needs. He disdains people who get their furniture from Ikea and buy Canadian brie and German prosciutto from Trader Joe's. He is certain that his girlfriends and clients are impressed by his lifestyle. You may be thinking Napoleon complex and you may be right.

Michael is such a good realtor that he assumes he is a financial genius. A lot of wealthy people think this way: if they are rich, they must be smart. Nope. There is a lot of luck in everyone's lives. People who make bad decisions tend to blame their failures on bad luck when it is often their own fault. People who are successful tend to underestimate the role of luck in their successes.

Michael blithely made many baffling financial decisions, but his mistakes were papered over by his high income. The truth was that he needed help and he was about to get some.

CHAPTER 11

Moon Cakes at Midnight

The moon has been an important part of Chinese culture for thousands of years, including the use of a lunar calendar, the association of rejuvenation with the moon, and the worship of Chang'e, the Moon Goddess of Immortality.

One of the most important Chinese holidays is the Mid-Autumn Festival (or Moon Festival), which occurs on the 15th day of the 8th moon of the lunar calendar. The moon is at its fullest and brightest and the timing coincides with the harvesting of many crops. Families gather for bonding, celebration, and a festival meal including traditional moon cakes eaten outdoors at midnight.

Lisa invited Jasmine to their family's Moon Festival and Jasmine accepted happily. There were duck, crab, and pork dishes along with many harvest foods, including pumpkins, taros, sweet potatoes, and dates. The mandatory mooncakes are pastries, that year filled with spiced walnut and red bean paste.

Partway through the festival meal, Michael announced that he had just invested in bitcoin and some other cryptocurrencies:

Prices have been going up several hundred percent a year and there's no risk because I bought several different cryptos. If one goes kaput, I'll still have the others.

Lisa was silent, but grimaced inside. Michael's infatuation with Bitcoin reminded her of their father's disastrous investment in Beanie Babies.

Jasmine kept her mouth shut, too, but was thinking,

There's nothing to keep any crypto from going kaput and, if one crypto does crash, they may all crash.

She tried to maintain a poker face, but was really bad at it. Michael noticed her skepticism:

What's wrong Jazz? Kicking yourself because you missed out on cryptomania?

Nope. Jasmine was just frustrated that so many otherwise intelligent people have been sucked into the crypto bubble. Cryptos aren't a real investment. They're just speculation, what economists call the Greater Fool Theory: buy something at a foolish price hoping to sell it to an even bigger fool for an even more foolish price. She wished that she had talked to Michael before he plunged.

She didn't want to ruin this time of bonding and celebration, so she simply said,

We just have different investment styles, that's all. I like to invest in things such as stocks and real estate that generate reliable income.

Michael smirked:

Boring. I prefer to double, triple, and quadruple my money so that I can buy more toys—such as the yellow Lamborghini I have my eye on.

Well, that doubled his foolishness in Jasmine's mind. She thinks that cryptocurrencies and yellow Lamborghinis are both a waste of money. She wanted to say something snippy, but she kept her mouth closed. She was the guest after all. Maybe if she acted civilized (even deferential), Michael might actually listen to her and not buy any more crypto—maybe even sell what he has while he can get a good price.

Lisa sensed what Jasmine was thinking and joined in the tag team. Instead of criticizing her brother directly, she reminded him of their father's obsession with Beanie Babies:

Remember when we were teenagers and dad spent thousands of dollars on Beanie Babies. They weren't really good for anything. We

weren't even allowed to play with them because they might get dirty or fall apart. All we could do with dad's Beanie Babies was put them in air-tight boxes in a dark closet.

Dad said they were our college tuition fund, but he would have been better off putting his money in a bank. He paid hundreds of dollars for some Beanie Babies that are now worth only hundreds of pennies.

If you want a good chuckle, go online and read the nonsense people post trying to find numbskulls to buy their Beanie Babies. Here's one I just found on my phone:

> The rarest and valuable beanie baby to ever exist!!! Princess, the purple bear was created to honor the memory of Princess Diana and very few were ever made and distributed. Features all tags and persevered in a corsage box. In pristine condition!!!

I wonder what this bear is "persevering" to do in a corsage box! They are offering this Beanie baby for $500,000, on sale from the normal $1 million price. Plus, the ad says that if you act quickly, the normal $7.95 shipping charge will be waived. Whoopee!

Lisa covered her mouth with her hand and said that she couldn't read this garbage without laughing.

Jasmine jumped back in:

Good luck with that sales pitch! I actually bought a Princess Beanie Baby recently, not as an "investment" but to put in my office and remind my clients of the perils of buying collectibles. I did have to pay $7.99 for shipping, but this was more than the cost of the bear.

Michael didn't appreciate Lisa's sarcasm, but he interpreted it as a swipe at their father, not himself. Dad had been listening, too, and he threw up his hands and gave out a big,

Ai Ya! Don't remind me.

He had never sold any of his Beanie Babies. It was just too painful to admit his terrible mistake.

Jasmine tip-toed into treacherous water, reminding herself constantly that she was the guest:

> *I'm sorry, but cryptocurrencies remind me of Beanie Babies. The only way to make money is to sell them to someone else for a higher price than you paid. With stocks and real estate, I don't have to worry about finding someone to sell them to. If I buy stocks or real estate at a favorable price, I will get plenty of income from the dividends and rent. In fact, if the price goes down, I will probably buy more.*
>
> *Right now, I'm getting $20,000 a year in rent net of the mortgage interest, property taxes, and other expenses from a condo I bought for $400,000. That's a 5 percent return and the rent will go up over time. If the market price of condos like mine drops to $200,000 and the rent is the same, I will buy another one and get a 10 percent return, and it will also grow over time.*

Michael scoffed,

> *Five percent? I guess that's fine if you're happy with 5 percent. I'm going for 100, 200, and 1,000 percent!*

Jasmine answered simply and softly because her goal was to persuade Michael, not provoke him:

> *Yeah, I wouldn't turn down a 100, 200, or 1,000 percent return, if it were guaranteed. My problem is that I don't feel the return is guaranteed if I have to count on selling it to someone else for 2, 3, or 10 times what I paid for it. With stocks and real estate, I don't worry about that because I know that I have the steady income and there is no pressure to sell. I like that serenity.*

Michael was still skeptical:

And I'm thinking that a 5 percent return is hardly worth the bother. You might as well put your money in a time capsule and open it when you're an old lady.

Jasmine kept her cool:

Yeah, I know 5 percent doesn't sound like much, but it does add up. That 5 percent return on my condo doesn't include the growing rent over time. If we take the rent growth into account, my annual return might be 8, 9, or 10 percent.

In addition, there's something called the "power of compound interest." If you start with $100,000 and earn, say, 10 percent, every year, you will earn $10,000 the first year. The second year, you will earn a 10 percent return on your initial $100,000 plus a 10 percent return on the $10,000 you earned the first year. Your return the second year will not be $10,000 but $11,000. This compounding of interest on interest can add up pretty fast. A compounded 10 percent return will double your money in a little over seven years.

Jasmine took a breath in order to let that sink in, and then pushed on:

There's this cool compounding rule of thumb called the Rule of 72. If you divide 72 by your annual rate of return, that tells you about how long it takes to double your money. With an 8 percent return, you will double your money in just nine years. With a 9 percent return, it will take only eight years. With a 10 percent return, 7.2 years.

She added the clincher:

Another thing is that $20,000 in annual income on a $400,000 condo would be a 5 percent return if I paid cash for the condo. I didn't. I only put $100,000 down and borrowed the rest. A $20,000 profit on my $100,000 investment is actually a 20 percent return. At that rate, I will double the value of my investment every three-and-a-half years and have nearly $100 million in 30 or 40 years. I'm going to be a rich old lady!

Jasmine could tell that Michael was getting interested, but that others were getting bored and wanted to go back to talking about sports, politics, and Chinese television shows:

Hey, Michael, I'm monopolizing the conversation and others are getting tired of listening to me yada, yada. Why don't we meet for coffee or lunch and I'll tell you more about why I love stocks and real estate.

Michael said *yes* and he wasn't just being polite. Jasmine had sunk a hook.

CHAPTER 12

Home for Rent, Home for Rent

Sure enough, Michael called Jasmine early Monday morning and suggested they meet at a local coffee shop known for its dark coffee and dark chocolates—two of Jasmine's favorite things in the world. How could she say no?

Jasmine had been thinking about what she would say to Michael and if she should show him some numbers, like a spreadsheet. His resistance to the idea that real estate is an investment is not surprising, but certainly seemed ironic. After all, he is a hotshot realtor, closing deal after deal, but he had never thought of buying a house as an investment. "A house is just a place where you live and everybody has to live somewhere, right?"

That myopia is not surprising. Most homeowners feel exactly the same way. On the other hand, it's ironic because Michael (and certainly realtors who aren't as smooth as Michael) could use the real-estate-as-an-investment argument to persuade reluctant homebuyers to sign on the dotted line.

Jasmine decided that a few numbers would help make her case, so she prepared some—not a mind-numbing spreadsheet with hundreds of eye-squint numbers, but a simple table that was easy to read and easy to understand.

Jasmine got to the coffee shop and there was no sign of Michael. She soon learned that he hates wasting time and, so, is seldom on time. Jasmine remembered back to when she was a kid playing on her high school soccer team, and the coach was fond of saying,

> *If you're 10 minutes early, you are on time. If you're on time, you're late. If you're late, you don't play.*

Michael is the opposite: If you show up 10 minutes early, then you're going to waste 10 minutes. He would rather sprint through an airport terminal trying to board a plane just before the doors close than get to the airport early and waste time waiting for boarding to start. When it comes to meetings, his perspective is that, if you're the top dog, then the meeting starts when you show up—not a minute sooner or a minute later. So, be the top dog. That he was.

Jasmine didn't mind him being late to their meeting. It gave her time to savor her coffee and a chocolate and think quietly about what she could say to convince Lisa's know-it-all brother.

Twenty minutes later, Michael walked through the door and headed to the coffee bar,

Hi Jazz! Sorry I'm late.

Jasmine's mind said, "Bullshit." Her mouth just smiled and said softly,

No worries.

She did wonder why Michael kept calling her Jazz instead of Jasmine. Was this some power trip to belittle her? No matter, if he felt a need to belittle her, that's his problem.

Once Michael had his coffee and a scone and sat down across from her, Jasmine said, "Long time," which she intended to be a joke to lighten the mood. He just nodded, "Yep."

Well, best to get to it. Jasmine started her pitch:

Everyone, especially a top realtor like you, understands that rental properties are an investment. People buy them to make a profit. What sometimes gets overlooked, though, is the power of leverage.

Like I said at the Moon Festival dinner, I'm currently getting $20,000 in annual income, after deducting mortgage payments, property taxes, and other expenses, on a condo I just bought for $400,000. It sounds like a 5 percent return, but I have 4-to-1

leverage because the price of the condo is four times the $100,000 that I actually invested. This means that my return is multiplied by 4. The $20,000 income is a 5 percent return on $400,000, but a 20 percent return on my $100,000 investment.

Michael seemed to agree so Jasmine went on:

I know rental properties are messy. You have to screen the renters, make sure they pay on time, and worry about repairs. I found a great property-management company that takes care of all that for me. They charge 10 percent of the monthly rent, but they're pros at this and I have better things to do with my time. You will probably feel the same way if you decide to buy some rental properties.

She had snuck in the hint that Michael might want to invest in a rental property and she made it plural ("properties") to sink the hook deeper. Jasmine went on:

I just add the management fee to the list of costs, along with mortgage payments, property taxes, insurance, maintenance, and so on, and see if the net income is large enough to justify buying the property.

Michael obviously understood, so Jasmine added,

The kicker is the leverage. There are very few investments that have stable income and such enormous leverage. With your reputation and income, banks might loan you money to buy rental properties with only 10 percent down, which would give you 10-to-1 leverage. A 5 percent profit on a property would then be a 50 percent profit on your investment!

Jasmine again made it plural ("properties") to suggest that it wasn't a question of whether to invest in a rental property, but how many properties to invest in. Subtly referring back to the Moon Festival skepticism about cryptocurrencies, she added,

Besides the leverage factor, the great thing about real estate is that a good rental property will generate terrific monthly income. You don't have to sell the property to make a profit.

If the rental income increases over time (as it almost surely will), the value of the property will increase too and you may, at some point, want to sell the property for a nice profit, but the crucial point is that you are not counting on selling the property to give you your profit.

Michael was unusually quiet and surprisingly receptive. He had to make it all about himself, but that was okay with Jasmine. She wasn't trying to score debate points; she just wanted to help him make sensible investments.

Jazz, I know the Orange County real estate market better than anyone and I know properties that are going to be coming up for sale before they go on the market. I can grab the best ones for myself—and I will pay a fair price because I need to protect my reputation.

And you're right, I know some banks that will be happy to loan me money to buy these properties because they know how much income I make and that I won't overpay for a property.

Jasmine didn't want to press her luck so she kept the tables of numbers that she had prepared inside her briefcase and postponed a discussion of how buying a house to live in is also an investment:

Great coffee. Great chocolate. Great talk. If you have time next week, I want to run another real estate idea by you and see what you think.

She knew that the next step was going to be tougher so she made it seem that Michael was helping her, rather than vice versa. He fell for it:

Sure Jazz. Happy to help. How about next Monday?

CHAPTER 13

Your Home Is an Investment

Next Monday came and Jasmine was back at her favorite coffee shop, waiting for Lisa's brother, Michael. She knew that this was going to be a harder sell so she planned her pitch carefully as she sipped her double espresso and munched on an espresso chocolate bar.

Michael showed up 20 minutes late, as expected, with a perfunctory, "Hi Jazz," as he headed for the coffee bar. Once he had his coffee and scone, he revealed that the meeting the previous Monday had indeed been a success:

> *No grass growing under my feet. I've had two offers accepted for condos near UCI. More than half the UCI students live off-campus—in part, because the college doesn't have enough housing for everyone and, in part, because students appreciate the freedom they have to eat what they want and do what they want without UCI monitoring them 24/7.*
>
> *The rent is great because some students are from wealthy families and other students don't mind sharing rooms with their friends.*
>
> *Also, it was easy for me to get 10 percent-down mortgages.*

Jasmine said, "Wow! Congratulations." She wasn't 100 percent certain that he had included all the expenses and she was near 100 percent certain that he hadn't thought about how rents will increase over time while his mortgage payments won't, making his returns even higher in the future than they are now, but that was okay. It was better to be conservative than aggressive.

Jasmine had written some software for taking growing rents into account, but she didn't want to upset Michael by suggesting that he might need her help. Instead, she switched to today's topic:

You know that list you made of the income and expenses from the rental properties you bought? That kind of list also applies to homes that people buy and live in themselves.

Michael looked skeptical, but Jasmine went on:

People who buy the homes they live in tend to think that their profit is the difference between the price they paid for the house and the price they sell it for: "I bought my house for $400,000 and sold it for $900,000; therefore, I made a half-million-dollar profit." There are so many things wrong with that claim that I hardly know where to begin.

Jasmine was pretty sure that Michael thought about houses that way, too, which is why she made it seem that she was talking about "other people."

Jasmine took out a sheet of paper and made a list of things wrong with "other people's" thinking. She started with the easy ones that Michael would quickly agree with:

1. *They are obviously ignoring leverage. How big is the profit relative to their investment? A half-million-dollar profit is more impressive if it is on a $100,000 investment than if it is on a $400,000 investment.*
2. *They are also ignoring the time frame: A half-million-dollar profit is more impressive if it is over 5 years than over 50 years.*

Jasmine said that these can be taken into account by calculating the annual percentage rate of return on the homeowner's investment. She doubted that Michael knew exactly how to do that, but she was confident that he got the point.

Then, Jasmine moved to the tough sell:

3. *The profits from a home a person lives in are very similar to the profits from a rental property. Most of the action is not from selling the house for a profit, but from the net monthly income.*

As she expected, Michael objected, "What income? When you live in your own home, all you have are expenses." Jasmine agreed (halfway):

You're right. When people try to figure out the rate of return on their homes, they should take into account all the expenses they incur: mortgage payments, property taxes, repairs, and so on.

But there is also income that they don't see—hidden income. They have to live somewhere and if they didn't own a home, they would have to pay rent. By owning the home they live in, they save those monthly rent payments—and a penny saved is a penny earned. Not paying a landlord $3,000 (or whatever) every month is like someone giving them $3,000 every month.

Then, she appealed to Michael's love of money:

In addition to showing potential homebuyers the prices of comparable homes and talking about how fast home prices are increasing in the area, you can talk about what a great return they are getting from the rent savings.

A lightbulb turned on. Michael knew that some buyers, especially those who had been renting for several years, would be receptive to this argument:

Make mortgage payments instead of rent payments! After years of renting, all a tenant has to show for it is rent receipts. After years of making mortgage payments, a homeowner has a house they can sell for a profit.

Michael loved it.

Jasmine was going to show Michael a table she had prepared with blank spaces for entering the income and expenses associated with home ownership, including the rent savings, so that he could help potential buyers calculate the annual profit from being a homeowner; then she remembered Lisa telling her that Michael isn't much of a numbers guy.

He doesn't close deals by showing his clients spreadsheets. He closes deals by being Peter Jennings, James Garner, and Michael J. Fox.

Jasmine kept her briefcase closed and grinned like a Cheshire cat, confident that she had gotten through Michael's protective shield of arrogance.

CHAPTER 14

Home Sweet Home

After each of Jasmine's Monday coffeeshop meetings with Michael, she would do an instant replay on Tuesday with Lisa. She didn't tell Lisa anything about Michael's personal situation, because that would have violated client confidentiality, but she taught Lisa the same principles she explained to Michael. Buying a home to rent or live in is a huge financial decision and Jasmine wanted to make sure that Lisa understood how to think about that decision correctly.

Lisa was far more receptive than her brother. She immediately understood about the importance of the rent savings and the need to consider all the expenses. Maybe she was smarter. More likely, Michael was skeptical about taking financial advice from a woman. Jasmine told Lisa that his disdain didn't matter to her:

If that's the problem, it's Michael's problem.

One reason Lisa was so receptive was that she had been thinking about buying a house for herself. When they divorced, Erik got the family home and Lisa got their vacation home in the mountains and some cash to even things out. Lisa sold the vacation property (too many memories) and had enough money for a down payment on a home in Irvine, near her parents and children. She hadn't been ready to make a commitment so she rented and waited.

Now, armed with what she had learned from Jasmine, she was ready to get serious. She knew from her brother Michael that,

The three most important things in real estate are location, location, location.

and she loved the location of the house she was renting.

It's in a quiet neighborhood and close to a large park that leads to wide, protected biking and walking trails. (Irvine has more than 100 miles of off-street bike trails and even more walking trails.) The home itself is 1,800 square feet, single-level, with two bedrooms, two bathrooms, and a large open floor plan that encompasses the kitchen, dining, and entertaining areas. The floors are white oak. The ceilings are high and the windows are massive.

The owner had decided to sell the house and was offering to sell it to Lisa for an even $1 million. Lisa had to make a decision—buy the house or move out.

She called Jasmine and told her that she wanted to talk about this decision at their next meeting. Lisa said that she would prepare for the meeting by making a list of income and expenses (money going in and money coming out) just like Jasmine had taught her:

The money coming is the rent savings; the money going out is the mortgage payments, property taxes, insurance, and maintenance.

Jasmine reminded her that,

If you itemize your deductions on your federal and California tax returns, the mortgage interest and property taxes will give you some tax savings.

The tax details are complicated, so one way to estimate the savings is to run whatever tax software you use two ways—with and without the mortgage interest and property taxes—and see what the difference is in your tax bill.

When she got home, Lisa constructed a table, including a line labeled "tax savings" and started filling in the numbers, with everything rounded to the nearest thousand dollars because of the inevitable uncertainties. Table 14.1 shows what she came up with.

Lisa did the calculations two ways—with a mortgage and without a mortgage. (She didn't really have enough money to buy the house without a mortgage, but she was curious what the numbers would look like.)

Lisa had been paying $4,000 a month ($48,000 a year), so the rent saving was straightforward. The first-year property tax would be 1 percent of the purchase price, so that's $10,000. She could add this property tax to her itemized deductions and save about $5,000 in Federal and California income taxes. She estimated that her annual home insurance would be $1,000 and the average annual maintenance expenses would be about $6,000.

The proverbial bottom line was a $36,000 profit. Jasmine calls the bottom line the "home dividend" to emphasize that it's comparable to dividends from stocks, so Lisa called it that, too. Relative to the $1 million cost of the house, the $36,000 first-year profit is a 3.6 percent after-tax return—which seemed okay but not great.

Lisa's table also showed the numbers if she were to put $250,000 down and take a 30-year $750,000 interest-only loan with a 4 percent interest rate. Jasmine pointed out that,

> *We can use our borrowing rule of thumb here. You are borrowing at 4 percent, but your combined federal and state marginal tax rate is roughly 50 percent. This means that, if you deduct the interest, your after-tax cost of borrowing is only about 2 percent, while the after-tax return on the house is 3.6 percent. Borrowing at 2 percent to invest at 3.6 percent will make the house an even better investment.*

Lisa nodded enthusiastically. She loved the rule of thumb and the numbers in her table confirmed that it worked. The annual interest would be $30,000 and the tax-deductibility of the interest would boost her tax savings from $5,000 to $20,000. The home dividend fell from $36,000 to $21,000 but now it's a return on her $250,000 down payment, instead of the $1 million price of the house. The after-tax rate of return jumped from a so-so 3.6 percent to a whopping 8.4 percent because borrowing at 2 percent to invest at 3.6 percent is a winning strategy.

Table 14.1 The first-year, after-tax home dividend for an Irvine home

	No Mortgage	Mortgage
Rent savings	48,000	48,000
Mortgage payments	0	−30,000
Property taxes	−10,000	−10,000
Tax savings	5000	20,000
Insurance	−1000	−1000
Maintenance	−6000	−6000
Home dividend	$36,000	$21,000
First-year return	3.6%	8.4%

Lisa concluded that,

With a mortgage, this home looks like a terrific investment.

She bought the house.

CHAPTER 15

This Old House

Shortly after Lisa bought her home in Irvine, she came to Jasmine with another real estate question:

My parents are thinking about adding an ADU to their home. I know this is a real estate question and that we should think about it the same way we think about buying a house, but I want to make sure I am doing it correctly.

ADU is the acronym for accessory dwelling unit, which is a separate living space with a private kitchen and bathroom for one, two, or even three people. Some ADUs are backyard cottages that are separate from the main house; others are attached to the main house and have their own entrances. They are often called "granny flats" because they can be used as separate living spaces for grandparents, children, or other relatives.

Many cities and states have relatively relaxed building restrictions and even offer financial incentives for building ADUs in order to increase the supply of affordable housing. Another great thing about ADUs is that they are relatively inexpensive to build because the owner does not have to buy any additional land and can often just remodel a garage or other already existing structure.

Lisa's parents had a three-car garage that was separate from their main house and they realized that they could make some steady rental income if they converted it to an ADU. They also thought it might be useful to have someone they trusted living on the property and keeping an eye on things when they were out of town. Their big question was whether it was worth the cost—would the rental income give them a good return on their investment?

Jasmine said,

That is a great question and, you're right, we can think of remodeling the same way we think about buying a house. I'm happy to help.

She added that remodeling questions come up all the time and it's always good to look at the financial ramifications:

We all change our minds. Conditions change. We change. Some of the reasons for remodeling are nonfinancial. A family that has more children needs more beds and may need another bedroom to put those beds in. A person who begins working from home may need an office to work in. An outdated kitchen may be inefficient and depressing. A swimming pool may be what the doctor ordered.

Those kinds of considerations are very personal in that the importance varies from person to person. However, there are financial considerations that apply to all remodeling decisions.

Jasmine knew from her Wharton training that there are two important economic principles to take into account.

One principle is to consider alternatives. A not-so-easy alternative to remodeling is to move—sell your current home and buy a new one. It sounds drastic but, sometimes, it is the best alternative.

Jasmine pointed out that there are costs in buying and selling a house (including daunting real estate commissions) and there are costs in moving one's belongings from one place to another, but there are also costs in remodeling, including the stress of dealing with contractors and living through the noise and mess. Sometimes, it is better to remodel; other times, it is better to move.

For your parents, moving is off the table. However, another alternative is to invest the money that would be spent on the ADU in the stock market. If the ADU doesn't generate a return comparable to stocks, then it would be a tough call, weighing the hassle of building an ADU with the benefit of having someone around to keep an eye on things.

Jasmine then turned to the second principle:

We should think on the margin: The relevant question is not how good things are or will be, but how much better or worse they will be than they are now.

Jasmine pointed out that, when people think on the margin, they are less susceptible to the *sunk-cost fallacy*, which is when we let our decisions be affected by things that happened in the past and cannot be changed.

Suppose you take advantage of a hot deal and buy a five-scoop ice cream cone. Three scoops in, you're feeling nauseous. A sunk-cost fallacy is to say, "I paid for five scoops and I need to eat all five scoops to get my money's worth." Thinking on the margin, the question is whether you would be better off eating the last two scoops or throwing them away.

Lisa nodded in agreement:

It seems totally obvious that we should not be swayed by things we can't change.

Jasmine was not surprised that Lisa understood immediately but she added,

Yep, in theory it's totally obvious. However, we all have memories and emotions and sometimes these trample rational thinking. For example, stock market studies have found that many professional investors take bigger risks after losing money, trying to win back what they lost. They know they should focus on the future, not the past, but they just can't help themselves.

Jasmine said that, for the ADU,

We should focus on the marginal costs and benefits: (a) the cost of converting your parents' three-car garage to a two-bedroom, one-bath ADU and (b) the monthly rental income, net of any ongoing expenses they might incur after construction.

They didn't assign any cost to the loss of the garage because Lisa's parents always parked their car outside in sunny Southern California. Lisa said,

Their garage is only used to store things that they should give away or throw away. If anything, it's probably a blessing to have a compelling reason to get rid of stuff they haven't looked at in years.

Lisa's parents found a reputable local contractor, looked at some of his projects, and talked to homeowners who had worked with him. He seemed competent and honest, and he got things done on time within budget. Perfect!

This contractor told them that the total cost, including material, labor, permits, and so on, would be $180,000. Lisa's parents had recently inherited some money and planned on paying cash for the conversion.

To estimate the benefits, Lisa considered the prospective rental income net of the increases in their property taxes, home insurance, and maintenance. She was careful to look at the marginal changes in their income and expenses.

California's Proposition 13, enacted in 1978, assesses a property at its market value when it is purchased and then limits the annual increases in assessed values to no more than 2 percent a year. It also limits the state property tax rate to 1 percent of the assessed value, though cities and counties can add additional levies if approved by two-thirds of their voters. Lisa assumed that the assessed value would increase by the $180,000 construction cost and be subject to a 1.3 percent property tax, growing by 2 percent a year.

Table 15.1 The first-year net income on Lisa's parents' ADU

Rent	36,000
Property tax	−2,340
Tax on rent	−10,400
Insurance	−250
Maintenance	−1,000
Net income	$22,010

She also estimated that their annual home insurance would go up by $250 the first year and that their maintenance expenses would increase by $1,000, with both growing by 3 percent annually. They would have to pay taxes on the rental income net of expenses, including the depreciation of the $180,000 cost over 27.5 years. Using some tax software, Lisa estimated that their total federal plus California income taxes would increase by about $10,400 the first year.

Table 15.1 shows that the anticipated first-year net income was $22,010 on their $180,000 investment, which is a first-year, after-tax return of 12.2 percent.

Jasmine added,

Not only that, over time, the net income will improve if the property tax grows by only 2 percent a year while the rent and other expenses increase by 3 percent annually.

Lisa said,

Yep, I thought of that. I also thought, using our borrowing rule of thumb, that my parents would do even better if they used borrowed money to pay part of the cost, but they are old school and very averse to borrowing.

Still, 12.2 percent is an excellent return. The contractor told Lisa's parents that he could begin building the ADU in May and be done by mid-August. They signed a $3,000/month 12-month lease with friends of friends, which would begin in September—and thanked Lisa for helping them decide to go ahead with the ADU.

CHAPTER 16

Good Day Sunshine

It wasn't long before another remodeling project was on the radar, one that was both simpler and more complicated than an ADU. This new project was simpler because there wasn't a long list of income and expenses, but it was more complex because there were additional factors to consider.

Month after month, Lisa had noticed that people were putting solar panels on their roofs. It seemed like a solar-panel competition. Who could put up the biggest and best-looking solar panels? She thought about joining the contest, but then remembered that she had sworn off buying things just for the sake of buying things.

Her decision should be strictly financial. Would solar panels reduce her electricity bills by more than the cost of installing the panels? That sure sounded like a home-remodeling project, very much like adding an ADU. She called Jasmine for advice and found herself being tested:

Yep, solar panels are just another home-remodeling project. I'm going to ask you to figure this one out on your own and get back to me for a double-check—though I am confident that you will do the analysis correctly.

Lisa did her due diligence, talking to the neighbors with solar-paneled houses about their experiences and she found broad agreement on one company that did good work installing quality panels at a fair price. No damaged roofs. No extra charges. No complaints whatsoever.

She called the company and got a price quotation for a system that seemed right for her home and lifestyle and also fit easily on the south-facing part of her roof. The system would produce 11,200 kilowatt-hours of electricity a year and cost around $18,000 to install, net of state and federal rebates. At the time, she was being charged about 30 cents per kilowatt hour for electricity, but she was using less than 11,200 kilowatt-hours per year. She could sell the excess back to the "grid" but at a bargain price. Overall, she estimated that the initial net savings would amount to around $3,000 a year, which is a 17 percent return on the $18,000 cost.

She called Jasmine and said that she was ready to show her the numbers. They met the following Tuesday at Jasmine's home and, after the usual hugs and greetings, they settled into the comfy chairs and Lisa shared her calculations with Jasmine, who was impressed with the research and the details but also said,

> *Now that you are the master of the plain-vanilla calculations, this is a great opportunity to talk about three other considerations. One thing that we've mentioned but done nothing about is that we should look beyond the first year because income and expenses generally increase over time. Here, electricity prices will almost surely go up and so will the savings from having solar panels. We should take that into account.*

Lisa quickly responded:

> *Yep, I've thought about that. In fact, I did a little research and the consensus seems to be that in the long run electricity prices will go up, on average, by about 4 percent a year, plus or minus 1 percent, but I don't know what to do with that information.*

Jasmine was pleased:

> *You are my star pupil. I will show you how to take that into account, but your research also revealed the second complication—uncertainty. We don't know whether the average rate of increase will be 3 percent, 4 percent, or 5 percent. Most financial calculations have uncertainties. One way to handle these uncertainties is to do the calculations for a range of plausible scenarios. Here, we can look at 3 percent, 4 percent, and 5 percent annual increases in electricity prices.*

Lisa nodded:

Makes sense. What's the third complication?

Jasmine responded:

Solar panels don't last forever. Maybe 20 to 25 years. Since this, too, is uncertain, we could consider both possibilities or, else, simply make the more conservative assumption that they will last 20 years.

Jasmine then invited Lisa to read a book or poke around outside while she ran some numbers on her computer. A half hour later, she returned with her results:

These calculations are tough to do on your own, but I wrote a computer program that can do the number-crunching we need. Remember when I mentioned "present value" a while back? The present value of money that is received in the future is how much that money is worth today, taking into account the fact that it could be invested if you have it today. Here, I calculated the total present value of all the projected electricity savings over the next 20 years. If this present value turns out to be more than $18,000, then the electricity savings—taking into account the time value of money— are larger than the cost of the panels.

Jasmine said that she assumed that the solar panels would last 20 years and that Lisa could earn a 7 percent return if she invested the $18,000 in something else (like stocks) instead of buying the solar panels. If electricity prices increase, as predicted, by 4 percent a year, the total present value of all the electricity savings over 20 years works out to be $45,557, well above the $18,000 cost of the solar panels. If electricity prices increase by only 3 percent a year, the present value is a tad lower, at $41,820. For a 5 percent annual increase in electricity prices, the present value is $49,736. Solar panels seemed to be a great investment even with the most conservative assumptions. Then, Jasmine said,

> *I want to show you one more cool thing. I can calculate the total present value for **any** rate of return you earn on your investments. Then we can see the rate of return you need to earn in order to beat solar panels.*

She showed Lisa the graph at the end of this chapter.

> *Here is what the graph looks like when we assume a 4 percent annual increase in electricity prices. The curved line is the present value of the electricity savings; the straight horizontal line is the $18,000 cost of the solar panels.*
>
> *You can see how far the present value is above or below the $18,000 cost for plausible rates of return on your other investments; for example, the present value is $45,557 with a 7 percent return.*
>
> *You can also see that the present value is above the cost of the panels for **any** rate of return below the breakeven rate of 21.8 percent. This means that unless you can earn more than 21.8 percent on your $18,000, you should invest in solar panels. For 3 percent and 5 percent annual increases in electricity prices, the breakeven rates of return are 20.6 percent and 23.0 percent, respectively. It seems that you should definitely invest in solar panels.*

That afternoon, Lisa called the solar-panel company and scheduled the installation.

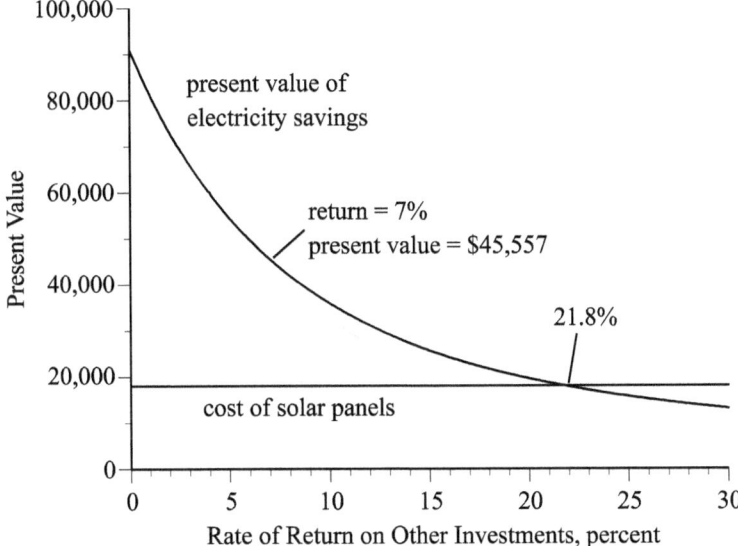

CHAPTER 17

Social Security

Lisa got an unexpected telephone call one morning from Uncle Andrew, an exuberant widower with no children—not that his exuberance is necessarily related to the absence of a wife and children. Uncle Andrew is an optometrist and, when he isn't working, spends most of his time playing Mahjong for money. Mahjong began in China and spread widely because of its alluring combination of simplicity and complexity. It is a classic game, like chess, that "takes minutes to learn and a lifetime to master."

The game is played with colorful tiles and straightforward rules, but the scoring is very complicated, verging on bewildering. Many beginners keep intricate scoresheets handy to remind them what various tile combinations are worth. Experts who know the scoring rules use flexible strategies based on this knowledge.

After looking at the initial tiles they have been dealt, experts identify the most promising ways to score points but, at this stage, leave many paths open. During the midgame, they modify their plans as the tiles drawn or discarded cause scoring opportunities to emerge and vanish. In the endgame, they focus on completing a winning hand before their opponents do. The cherry on top is that, while skill will triumph in the long run, the scores in individual games are largely determined by luck—which can be exhilarating.

When Lisa saw the caller ID that morning, she was more than a bit concerned because Uncle Andrew hardly ever phoned her. Hoping it wasn't bad news, Lisa answered his call quickly, "Hi Uncle Andrew. Is everything okay?" He answered with a chuckle, "Oh yes, I just wanted to run an idea by you."

Turns out he had read an interview with Laurence Kotlikoff, an economist who is most well-known for the financial advice he gives households. The interview was mostly about Social Security retirement benefits and, since Andrew was now 55, he thought he should start thinking about them. Lisa agreed but she also said,

> *I really think you should talk to my friend Jasmine. She's not only my friend; she's my financial guru. She helped my parents with the financials for their ADU, she helped me decide to buy a house and install solar panels, and she can help you with Social Security.*

Andrew asked what an ADU was and then readily agreed to talk to Jasmine. Lisa said that she would ask Jasmine to call him and she did so immediately after they said their goodbyes and hung up.

When Jasmine phoned, Andrew told her about the Kotlikoff interview and how, after reading the story, he had surfed the Internet looking for more advice about Social Security:

> *I used to cut interesting stories out of newspapers and magazines with scissors and save them in manila folders. Now I cut-and-paste Internet articles into digital folders labeled "automobiles," "healthy food," and so on. I created a new folder—"Social Security"—and it got big fast. There are LOTS of articles about Social Security and they sometimes give conflicting advice.*
>
> *I realized that I need to talk to an expert and Lisa told me that you're the one I should talk to, so here I am.*

Jasmine didn't make fun of Andrew's habit of collecting articles—she does the same thing. She was sitting near her computer, so she opened up her "Social Security" folder.

Jasmine said that one important thing about Social Security retirement benefits that a lot of people don't know is that you don't have to retire in order to start collecting benefits. She explained that the government has something it calls "full retirement age" which, for Andrew, is 67 years old. This doesn't mean that he should or must retire at 67. The full retirement age is just used to determine the size of the benefits. Andrew could retire from his job earlier, later, or never.

Andrew said that he had indeed figured that out from his web exploration. He had also discovered that the Social Security bureaucracy has an online benefits calculator. He typed in his information and found that if he starts collecting when he turns 67, his monthly benefits will be around $3,000 in today's dollars. If he delays the start of benefits past 67 to 68, 69, or 70, the size of his benefits will increase by 8 percent for every year he delays, which works out to be $3,240 if he starts at 68, $3,480 if he starts at 69, or $3,720 if he starts at 70. Andrew could also start collecting benefits earlier—as early as 62—but then his monthly benefits would be less than $3,000.

Kotlikoff and most of the other experts Andrew found on the Internet strongly advise people to wait until they are 70. For example, Andrew found this assertion by Mark Hulbert, a senior columnist for the financial website *MarketWatch*:

The nearly universal advice from financial planners is to delay claiming as long as possible.

When Andrew read the Hulbert quotation to Jasmine, she said:

Yep. I have the exact same quotation in my Social Security folder.

Another cut-and-paste clipping quoted Professor Kotlikoff (and two distinguished co-authors):

The vast majority of American workers should delay taking their retirement benefits until 70.

Specifically,

Virtually all U.S. workers ages 45–62 would benefit from waiting until age 65 to collect. More than 90 percent would benefit from waiting until age 70.

Andrew naturally concluded that he should listen to the experts and wait until 70. He was puzzled, however, because he also found several articles saying that 90 percent of all people start collecting before age 70;

indeed, the most popular starting age is 62! Are they knuckleheads? Or are the experts? Should Andrew start collecting at 62, instead of 70?

That was Andrew's question and, to his dismay, Jasmine's answer was, "It depends." When he was the president, Harry Truman lamented,

> *Give me a one-handed economist! All my economists say "on the one hand… [and then] on the other."*

Like most people, Truman didn't want to be given complicated, conflicting options. He wanted to be told what to do. Andrew felt the same way. He didn't want to make a decision, he wanted Jasmine to make the decision for him.

Unfortunately, Social Security rules are literally thousands of pages long and cover a blizzard of different situations including benefits for the spouses and children of retired workers, the spouses and children of deceased workers, and the parents of deceased workers. There is no universal best answer for when to begin collecting benefits. However, once Jasmine knew more about Andrew, she could help him make an informed decision.

Jasmine told Andrew that she could answer some of his questions over the phone, but they would also have to meet in person so that she could show him some calculations for his specific situation—with no spouse and no dependent children or parents.

Andrew agreed to meet with Jasmine but, first, he wanted to ask her if she agreed with all those experts who say that larger benefits are inherently better. Bigger is better, right? For example, a *Barron's* editor who focuses on retirement issues wrote that,

> *The first step is waiting as long as possible to claim Social Security… Your monthly benefit will rise by at least 76 percent if you claim at 70 instead of 62.*

Jasmine told Andrew that, sure, larger benefits are good but they come at a price. If Andrew waits past 67, until 70, his monthly Social

Security benefits will be $3,720 instead of $3,000. True enough, but the cost is that he will have to give up three years of $3,000 monthly benefits—a total of $108,000—to get that $720 monthly-benefit bump.

If he lives long enough, the higher monthly benefits will be worth the initial cost, but that was hardly a given. Jasmine told Andrew that "long enough" depended on the rate of return he can earn on the $108,000 and that she couldn't do the calculations in her head:

I'll run some numbers and show you if you come to my house tomorrow.

Andrew protested:

No, No, No. It's an easy calculation. I found several experts (including Professor Kotlikoff) saying that the 8 percent increase in benefits for each postponed year past 67 gives me a guaranteed 8 percent rate of return. Since I don't think I can get that good a return on my investments—certainly not a guaranteed 8 percent—postponing seems to be a no-brainer.

Andrew read Jasmine several of his electronic clippings:

Laurence Kotlikoff: *That's a safe real return of 8 percent. You can't get anything close to that in the market.*

Scott Tucker, Kiplinger Personal Finance: *If you wait to take your benefits until after your (full retirement age), Social Security will add an 8 percent delayed retirement credit to your eventual monthly payout each year you hold off, up until age 70. That's a guaranteed return of 8 percent per year.*

Bob Carlson, senior contributor, Forbes: *Between full retirement age and 70, the annual increase for delaying benefits is 8 percent per year, tax free. That's a steep hurdle for an investment strategy to clear.*

Yada, yada, yada. Jasmine wasn't surprised. She had those clippings, too. She told Andrew that,

This is certainly a seductive conclusion. Look how many smart people think it's true. But it isn't.

Jasmine remembered that when she first heard the 8 percent-guaranteed-return argument, she was tempted to agree but then she started thinking about it. It has the same cost–benefit problem as the bigger-is-better argument; it's just more subtle.

She explained her reasoning to Andrew:

*You won't be forgoing $3,000/month when you are 67 in order to get $3,240 when you are 68. You will be forgoing $3,000/month when you are 67 in order to get $3,240/month **instead of** $3,000/month when you are 68.*

Andrew seemed half-way persuaded—which was better than nothing but not good enough—so she tried to explain it another way:

You are giving up $3,000/month when you are 67 to gain an extra $240/month when you are 68. If you happen to die when you are 69, your effective annual rate of return is negative 92 percent. Your return will eventually turn positive as you get older but, and you have to trust me on this, you cannot live long enough for the return to be 8 percent.

Andrew is smart—most optometrists are—so Jasmine tried to explain the time value of money, another core principle for financial decisions:

In addition, the dollars you give up when you are 67, 68, and 69 are a lot more valuable than the extra dollars you will get when you are 70, 80, or 90 because the sooner you get the money the sooner you can invest it and make more money. The only way to compare

dollars today with dollars tomorrow is to do some calculations like the ones that I will show you tomorrow.

These calculations are not trivial, but Lisa owed Andrew a favor (don't ask) and Jasmine was curious, too, because she would have to make a similar decision at some point.

Andrew was on board. He thanked Jasmine (and meant it) and said he looked forward to seeing her and her numbers the next day. Jasmine was also eager to see how they would turn out, so she did the calculations shortly after their call ended. She also invited Lisa to the next day's get-together because Jasmine was certain she would be interested, too.

The Next Morning

When Andrew and Lisa showed up the next morning at Jasmine's house, Jasmine reminded Andrew of some of the things they had talked about the previous afternoon—in part to jog his memory and, in part, to bring Lisa up to speed.

Jasmine also told them both that,

There are two factors that determine the best starting date. The first is how long you will live; the longer you live, the more it pays to postpone in order to get higher benefits over many, many years. The second factor is the rate of return you earn on your benefits; if you start taking benefits early and invest them wisely, you might have a lot more money than if you wait to start receiving benefits.

Andrew and Lisa both nodded enthusiastically.

Andrew planned on living a long time and this optimism nudged him toward waiting for higher benefits:

I'm in great health. I don't eat a lot of junk food and I'm a big believer in the mantra, "Exercise is medicine," which means that if you exercise regularly, you are less likely to get sick and need medicine. The official recommendation is at least 150 minutes a week and I play squash Monday, Wednesday, and Friday and go on two 20-miles-plus bike rides every weekend, so I'm far beyond 150 minutes.

Lisa said,

On the other hand, accidents do happen. Even healthy people can get sick or get in accidents. Bike riders, in particular, can have accidents. I imagine that you are an aggressive rider—and aggressive riders sometimes take spills. I have a friend who used to ride professionally. He once told me that he had had 14 bicycle accidents. When I said that seemed like a lot, he replied that he was only counting serious accidents where he had broken some bones or been banged up pretty badly.

She didn't need to tell Andrew that life is fragile. He lost his wife when a drunk driver plowed into her sports car. There is no guarantee that Andrew or anyone else will live to any particular age.

As for the second factor, the rate of return on investments, Andrew said,

I'm a very good investor, so I should probably start collecting my benefits early. The sooner I can get my hands on government money, the more money I can make.

Jasmine saw Andrew and Lisa's brains whirring, wondering which was more important—living long or investing wisely. Jasmine said,

I know what you're thinking. That is the right question and this is why I made a simple table that can help us all assess the dueling consequences of living a long life and making good investments.

Here is the table Jasmine handed to Andrew and Lisa. It combines these two competing factors by showing, for different investment returns, how long Andrew would have to live in order for postponing benefits to be worth it.

Minimum age at death to justify postponing benefits

Inflation-Adjusted Rate of Return	Start at 67 Instead of 62	Start at 70 Instead of 67
0%	79	82
2%	81	85
5%	88	92
8%	>120	>120

The first column gives different values for the rate of return on Andrew's investments. Social Security benefits are adjusted for inflation so we have to use an inflation-adjusted investment return, which is the rate of return minus the rate of inflation. If Andrew earns a 7 percent return on his investments and the rate of inflation is 2 percent, then his inflation-adjusted return is 5 percent.

The second column shows how long Andrew has to live for a decision to postpone benefits until age 67 instead of 62 to pay off. For example, if Andrew earns a 5 percent inflation-adjusted return, then he has to live to 88 for the higher benefits from starting at 67 to offset the 5 percent return on benefits starting at 62. The average 62-year-old U.S. male lives to 81; only 25 percent make it to 88. (The odds are better for 62-year-old females, who live, on average, to 84, with 38 percent living to 88.)

The third column shows how long Andrew has to live for a decision to postpone benefits until 70 instead of 67 to pay off. For a 5 percent return, he has to live to 92 for postponement to be profitable. The average 67-year-old U.S. male lives to 83; only about 13 percent make it to 92. (The average 67-year-old female lives on average, to 85, with 22 percent living to 92.)

Andrew is a smart guy and he studied the table for several minutes. Finally, he said,

All the minimum ages for starting at 70 are higher than the minimum ages for starting at 67. So, people who don't live long enough to benefit from postponing until 67 also don't live long

enough to benefit from postponing until 70. If 62 is better than 67, it is also better than 70.

Then, he reached the same conclusion that Jasmine had reached:

Those so-called experts are the knuckleheads. Maybe postponement until 70 makes sense for many gals and for guys who live well past their life expectancy, but most men don't live long enough for postponement to pay off.

Bingo!

Jasmine also cautioned that people who are bad investors would not benefit much from collecting early benefits. Andrew was confident that he could earn at least a 5 percent return and that he would most likely live to 88, but he wasn't convinced that he would live to 92. So, his tentative plan was to start collecting at 67, but he would make a final decision shortly before he turned 62, based on his health and his investment performance. Lisa was thinking the same thing except she expected to live longer than Andrew. She, too, would not make a final decision until she was older and knew more about her health at that time, but 67 seemed to be a reasonable choice.

Jasmine had not wanted to overcomplicate things, but now she added another often-decisive reason for not starting at 62:

If you start collecting benefits before 67 and are still working, you lose $1 in benefits for every $2 you earn above an annual limit ($21,240 in 2023).

That sealed the deal. Age 67 was the tentative winner for both Andrew and Lisa.

While they all drank celebratory double espressos, Jasmine told them that other situations are even more complicated:

Some people (not you two) don't have enough income or assets to buy the food or shelter they need, so they start their Social Security benefits as soon as they can. On the other hand, delaying benefits may protect people (not you two) from making foolish decisions like squandering their Social Security income on unnecessary frivolities instead of investing their benefits prudently.

Another complexity is that if you were married, either you or your spouse would be entitled to spousal benefits equal to up to half the size of the other person's full-retirement benefits and survivor benefits equal to 100 percent of the benefits their spouse was receiving when they died. Married couples have to think about their joint life expectancy.

Andrew said that his head was spinning. Lisa agreed and even Jasmine had to admit that she was feeling a bit woozy—and it wasn't from the double espresso. She said that,

Complicated situations require complicated tables, but the principles are exactly the same: compare both the costs and benefits and take into account the time value of money. If either of you remarry, we'll revisit Social Security.

CHAPTER 18

Other Retirement Accounts

At their next meeting, Jasmine began by saying that they should follow up their Social Security discussion by talking about other retirement plans:

> *I know, I know. We both hope that you will find a job that you love so much that you may never retire. I certainly don't plan on retiring. Even so, there can be a huge financial benefit from putting money into a retirement plan—even if you never retire. The reason is TAXES. You probably don't like thinking about taxes—I know I don't—but it pays to be smart about them and retirement plans can have terrific tax benefits.*

Jasmine then said she had to give Lisa a little background. It used to be that most workers' pension plans paid retirement benefits based on their income before they retired and how many years they had worked for the company. For example, someone who had worked for a company for 30 years and was making $5,000 a month might be paid a lifetime pension of $3,000 a month.

> *It sounds nice but there were problems—even shenanigans. For example, some companies didn't put enough money aside to pay the promised benefits. If the company went bankrupt, their employees lost their pensions.*
>
> *Also, if employees had to work for a company for, say, 30 years or past the age of 60 in order to qualify for benefits, some unscrupulous companies fired workers before they hit these benchmarks. They got no pensions at all!*
>
> *Even if the company wasn't being a complete monster, these pension plans handcuffed workers to their jobs. If you have to work*

for a company for 30 years to qualify for retirement benefits, then it's pretty expensive to leave and take a job with another company before you've put in your 30 years. The same is true if the benefits escalate the longer you work for a company. The bosses know this, of course, so they give you small raises and onerous tasks, confident that you won't tell them to "take this job and shove it."

Lisa grimaced and Jasmine went on to explain that these are called *defined-benefit plans* because they specify the size of the monthly retirement benefit. For several years now, many companies have been taking a completely different approach: *defined-contribution plans* in which workers and companies put money into an employee's own personal retirement fund.

Lisa interrupted,

That's exactly what my company has. I can put up to 10 percent of my salary into my 401(k) and the company matches it dollar-for-dollar. If I quit and take a new job, it's my money and it goes with me.

Jasmine quickly responded,

That is what I am talking about.

My mom and dad were both college professors and they had similar plans funded by the colleges they worked for and administered by a company named TIAA. They worked at three different colleges and they each had three different retirement plans, all under the TIAA umbrella.

Matching plans are pretty common and I'm confident that you have been putting the maximum amount into your plan because dollar-for-dollar matching is essentially free money. You'd be surprised, though, how many people don't do this. They would rather spend a dollar than put two dollars in their retirement plan.

She added,

Even if there isn't employer matching, there is a compelling argument for putting money in a retirement plan, either an employer-sponsored plan or an individual retirement account (IRA) that people can set up on their own if they don't have an employer plan or earn a lot less than you do. It's all about taxes.

Jasmine explained that when you put money into a 401(k) or an IRA, you postpone the taxes on that income. If your annual income is $100,000 and you put $10,000 into a 401(k) or an IRA, you only pay taxes on $90,000 now, and then pay taxes on that $10,000 (plus whatever it has earned) when you take your money out of the plan.

Lisa interrupted,

And you will probably be in a lower tax bracket when you are retired than you are now!

Jasmine responded,

True but, believe it or not, postponing taxes is profitable even if your tax rate is the same when you take money out as it was when you put money in.

Lisa said,

Wait a minute, wait a minute. That flew right over my head.

Jasmine smirked,

Yup, that's a tricky one. Remember the time value of money? It's better to pay your taxes later than to pay them now.

Let's do an example. To make it really simple, suppose that you are in a 50 percent tax bracket and your employer offers you a choice: (a) put $10,000 of your income into your 401(k) for one year; or (b) pay you $10,000 normally, with you paying $5,000 in taxes and investing the remaining $5,000 for one year. Either way, we'll assume that you earn a 10 percent return on your investment.

For your 401(k), you will have $11,000 at the end of the year and, if you take your money out of the plan and are still in a 50 percent tax bracket, you will pay $5,500 in taxes and have $5,500 left over. For the second strategy, you don't have to pay taxes on the $5,000 you invested, but you do have to pay taxes on the 10 percent return. If you bought stocks, for example, even with a favorable 15 percent tax on the dividends and capital gains, your after-tax return is only 8.5 percent, leaving you $5,425 instead of $5,500.

Bottom line: A stock investment that earns 8.5 percent outside a retirement plan would earn 10 percent if it was inside a retirement plan. It doesn't seem like much after one year, but we know from the miracle of compound interest that the difference between a 10 percent return and an 8.5 percent return over 20, 30, or 40 years is enormous. After 30 years, for example, we're talking about $174,494 versus $115,583. The difference is even larger if you invest in bonds or something else that has a higher tax rate.

Lisa said, "Wow," and Jasmine said,

There is a little bit more. I should also tell you about a special kind of IRA, called a Roth IRA.

Lisa said,

I've heard of these, but I have no idea what makes them special.

Jasmine laughed:

Allow me....
    You put after-tax dollars in a Roth IRA, which would be $5,000 in our example, but then there are no more taxes—not on the $5,000 or on the income and the capital gains you earn inside the Roth. If you earn a 10 percent return, it is a 10 percent after-tax return.
    A Roth, 401(k), and traditional IRA do equally well if your tax rate when you take money out is the same as when you put money

in. *The Roth wins if your retirement tax rate is higher and the Roth loses if your retirement tax rate is lower. So that is one thing to think about.*

Another consideration is that a 401(k) and traditional IRA have required minimum distributions (RMDs) that begin at age 73. These force you to take money out of your retirement plan and pay taxes on these withdrawals. If you die before all the money is withdrawn, your beneficiaries are also subject to (complicated) RMD rules. A Roth IRA is different. There are no RMDs for the owner of the account or for a spouse that inherits the account. After the spouse dies, there is a requirement that the account be emptied within 10 years—but having an extra 10, 20, or more years of tax-free returns is a big deal, which is why I am a huge fan of Roths.

Lisa said,

Well, now I am too.

Jasmine said,

And well you should be. The only problem is that Roths are so darn attractive that the government limits how much people can put in a Roth, especially high-income earners like you. In fact, your income is so high that you are not allowed to put ANY money directly into a Roth IRA.

There is a strategy called a "Backdoor Roth" where you put after-tax money in a traditional IRA and then transfer it to a Roth, but the IRS may clamp down on this workaround and even impose penalties.

It's almost like a whack-a-mole game where government tax lawyers set the rules; private tax lawyers find loopholes in the rules; government tax lawyers close these loopholes; and private tax lawyers find new loopholes. It generates plenty of income for tax lawyers, but drives the rest of us crazy.

Lisa said,

Ouch! I don't want to play whack-a-mole and I'm not looking for audits or penalties. Not that I've done anything wrong, but I don't want to waste my time dealing with the IRS.

Jasmine said,

I agree, so let's just put as much money as we can into your company's 401(k).

CHAPTER 19

Life Insurance

Austin (one of Lisa's cousins) called Jasmine one day because she and her husband Dallas (No, she wasn't joking) were thinking about buying life insurance. They both were 25, and a nice man they met at a party told them that they could save a lot of money on life insurance by locking in the monthly payments (called premiums) while they are young and healthy. Older people naturally have to pay a lot more every month because their chances of dying are so much higher.

Jasmine hid her wariness and said that she could indeed offer advice—advice that might surprise them—but she would have to charge them for it. After Austin agreed, Jasmine asked her if she had any numbers they could work with. She did:

I called the party guy (Robert) the next day and he quoted me some appealing prices, though we would both have to pass a mandatory medical examination—which shouldn't be a problem. We both exercise regularly and are in excellent health.

A plain-vanilla $1 million whole-life insurance policy for Austin would cost $660 a month and pay her beneficiaries $1 million when she died. A similar policy for Dallas would cost a bit more ($765 a month) because men tend to die younger. Austin enthusiastically blurted out,

It seems like a great deal! Robert told me that the average American 25-year-old female lives to 82 and the average American 25-year-old male lives to 78. If we live to our life expectancies, the $1 million payout will be more than double the amount we will have paid in premiums. It's not only a great investment, but we will have the security of knowing that one of us (or our children, if we ever have any) will get $1 million when either of us dies!

Jasmine sighed. Another time-value-of-money misconception. The premiums paid now are a lot more valuable than a payout received 50-plus years from now. She warned Austin,

I can tell you are excited, but let me do some calculations and I'll call you right back.

Twenty minutes later, she called with the deflating news:

These policies have been priced so that if you live to your life expectancy (82 for Austin, 78 for Dallas) your rate of return will be 2.5 percent, which is pretty puny in a world where Treasury bonds pay twice that and stocks have historically yielded about a 10 percent return.

Jasmine went on to explain that their returns would be a little higher (3 percent) if they died five years before their life expectancy and little lower (2 percent) if they lived five years beyond their life expectancy: "You're basically making a bet that you will die young and, even then, the return is lousy."

Austin asked Jasmine how much better off they would be if, instead of buying life insurance, they invested the premiums every month and earned a 5 percent return. Jasmine was prepared for exactly that question and would have asked it herself if Austin hadn't:

You'll have $1 million by age 65, $2.5 million if you live to your life expectancy of 82 years, and $3.7 million if you live to 90. Dallas will have $1 million by 63, $2.3 million if he lives to his life expectancy of 78 years, and $4.3 million if he lives to 90.

Then, Jasmine gave the punchline:

You're basically betting that you will die before 65 and Dallas is betting he will die before 63.

Jasmine had another arrow in her quiver. She went on:

If you earn a better return by investing in stocks, say 7 to 10 percent, then life insurance is a bet you will die in your 50s—which isn't darn likely.

Austin was puzzled:

Did you check your calculations. If they are right, then why do so many people buy life insurance?

Jasmine told her that she had checked and double-checked the numbers and the bottom line didn't surprise her at all:

Insurance companies invest the premiums you pay them so that they will have more than enough money to pay their claims when they come in. They set the size of their premiums pretty high so that they will make a profit even if they don't earn a great return when they invest the premiums. If they are making money, on average, then their customers are losing money, on average. This means that the average person who buys life insurance would do better investing the premiums at even modest rates of return.

Jasmine did admit that,

With all insurance, there are some people who have a better-than-average chance of collecting. Some people have health problems, but are nonetheless able to buy medical insurance at premiums set for people in good health. Some people may not be safe drivers, but can buy car insurance at premiums set for good drivers. Some people may be sickly, but can buy life insurance at premiums set for people with average life expectancies.

As far as I know, none of these apply to you and Dallas. You both seem to be in great health and have a lot of long-lived ancestors.

Jasmine also acknowledged that there are situations where life insurance might make sense if an untimely death would leave a family with no income or assets:

> *But that's not the case for you and Dallas. The death of either of you would be emotionally devastating, but not financially ruinous—because both of you are working and (I hope) saving some of your income to buy stocks and bonds for a time when either or both of you retire.*
>
> *This is why it seldom makes sense for a child, a senior citizen, or another family member to buy life insurance if they are not working and do not have other people dependent on their income.*

Jasmine's recommendation was for Austin and Dallas to save and invest, and not buy life insurance.

CHAPTER 20

Annuity Snake Oil

Lisa phoned Jasmine one day to tell her that her Aunt Marie had been mailed a fancy "personal invitation" to a free dinner and informative financial seminar at Mama Mia's, a local Italian restaurant. Lisa said that she warned Marie:

I've told her over and over that there's no such thing as a free lunch, but she just joked that she was getting a free dinner, not a free lunch. Marie had wanted to try the food at Mama Mia's for quite a while and now it was free.

Marie went to the dinner and told me afterward that the decor was cheesy and the food was so-so at best—a limp salad, overcooked pasta, and watered-down drinks that cost extra. The presentation, however, was top-notch—a well-dressed, dynamic young man with nice hair and slick slides.

Jasmine said simply,

Oh boy! Bring her to my house and we'll straighten this out.

When Lisa and Marie arrived at Jasmine's house, Jasmine was not at all surprised that the dinner topic had been annuities. Marie said that,

Here's how it works. I give the young man's company some money and they give me monthly income for as long as I live. That's right. Even if I live to 80, 90, or 100, the monthly checks keep coming.

Marie had scribbled down the young man's telephone number during the presentation and, when she phoned him the morning after the free dinner, she learned that,

> *For $1 million, I can buy an annuity that will give me a 6 percent annual return, which is $60,000 a year or $5,000 a month, for as long as I live. I'm not getting anything close to 6 percent on my stock portfolio—only about 1 to 2 percent each year in dividends. A 2 percent return on a $1 million stock portfolio is only $20,000.*

Jasmine was disappointed but she didn't let Lisa or Marie know that. Jasmine knew that there is a common confusion between making a profit on an investment and selling part of an investment, and that annuity salespeople can exploit this confusion.

A large part of that $60,000 annual payout would effectively just be the company giving Marie back part of the $1 million she paid the company:

> *Marie, that charming sales guy is misleading you. If you really were getting a 6 percent return, you would get $60,000 every year and still have $1 million left to give your heirs when you die. But you won't. When you die, that $1 million is gone.*

She told Marie that one thing people can be confident of when they buy insurance, annuities, or other financial products is that the company selling the products expects to make a profit—and their profits come out of their customers' losses. She told Marie that she would probably be better off if she cut the company out of the equation and created her own "homemade annuity":

> *If you hold on to your $1 million, you can use the dividends and some annual stock sales to give yourself $60,000 every year and you will probably have money left over for your heirs when you die— because the insurance company isn't taking a cut of the action.*

Jasmine asked Marie how old she was (65), and then asked her to enjoy a cup of coffee or glass of wine while she made some quick calculations. Marie and Lisa both chose coffee—it was 8:30 in the morning, after all—while Jasmine went to her computer.

Jasmine had written a computer program that does the calculations she needed and she was back with Marie and Lisa before they had finished their coffee. Jasmine told Marie that,

> *The average 65-year-old American woman lives a bit less than 20 years. If you live 20 years—until you are 85—the rate of return on your $1 million annuity will only be 1.88 percent. This means that if you skip the annuity and invest the $1 million yourself and earn more than 1.88 percent, you will have money left over when are 85.*

Jasmine knew that the annual return on U.S. Treasury bonds was 5 percent at that time so she told Marie that if she invested her $1 million in bonds paying 5 percent, she would have nearly $600,000 of her $1 million left when she was 85 and nearly $200,000 left if she lived to 95. Jasmine explained:

> *Think about it. A 5 percent return on $1 million is $50,000. If you spend $60,000 that first year, you only need to sell $10,000 of your $1 million bond portfolio. As your bond portfolio shrinks, you will have to sell more bonds to get your annual $60,000, but you won't run out of money unless you live to 99.*

Jasmine knew Marie was thinking that she might live past 99 so she added,

> *There is a small chance you will live to 99. But this $1 million isn't all you have. It's not like you will be sleeping on the streets if you live to 100. You have a mortgage-free house, monthly Social Security benefits, and a bunch of stocks. Worse comes to worse, you're a nice lady and I'm sure your children, grandchildren, and great-grandchildren would be honored to help out if you need it.*
>
> *It is certainly true that there is some peace of mind knowing that the annuity payments will last your entire life, but you pay dearly for that comfort. Most people will have literally hundreds of thousands of dollars for bequests if they don't buy an annuity.*

Jasmine also pointed out that there was no reason why she had to invest the entire $1 million in Treasury bonds. Highly rated corporate bonds give even higher rates of return and the average return on stocks over the next 20 to 40 years would almost surely be higher still.

Lisa and Marie were both quiet and Jasmine knew they were processing this data dump. Then, Marie blurted out,

Why was that nice young man peddling snake oil?

Jasmine didn't know how to say it nicely so she simply said,

That's what they are paid to do. If you buy a million-dollar annuity, he will get at least a $20,000 commission, maybe more. How do you think he paid for the "free" dinner? All he has to do is sell one annuity and it will be well worth his time and the cost of the meals.

Jasmine saw Marie grimace and continued,

Don't beat yourself up. A lot of people buy annuities because they have no idea how terrible the implied returns are.

She added,

I apologize for my blunt language. I get really steamed when a company—not just financial companies, any company—tries to take advantage of people's ignorance. Insurance companies could increase the rate of return on annuities and still make a good profit. The only reason they pay such lousy returns is because they can get away with it.

Jasmine then tried to calm Marie's indignation by explaining another reason why annuities are such a bad deal:

When you buy life insurance, the company usually requires a medical examination because they don't want to pay early because

you die early. Health exams aren't required for annuities because the company makes more money if you die early.

Jasmine went on to explain that this is an example of what economists call *asymmetric information*—you know more about your health than does the company selling annuities. This imbalance leads to another bit of economic jargon—*adverse selection*. People in good health who expect to live a long time are more likely to buy annuities than are people in poor health.

Once upon a time, the British government sold annuities that did not depend on the age of the purchaser! Can you guess what happened? There was adverse selection in that the annuities were a bargain for young people and mainly purchased by young people.

Jasmine told Marie that modern companies don't make that colossal mistake. They price annuities based on age (the younger you are, the more you pay) and, because the companies can't tell who is in good health and who isn't, they assume that everyone buying annuities is in good health and price them accordingly:

This makes annuities an especially bad deal for people who are unlikely to live well past their life expectancy—people who are in poor health or inherited bad genes.

Lisa reminded Marie that both of her parents died in their early 80s:

I'm not saying that you are destined to die young. I am saying that you are almost certainly better off investing your $1 million on your own.

Jasmine thought,

I couldn't have said it better.

CHAPTER 21

Peaceful Place

At their next meeting, Lisa said that all this talk about Social Security, life insurance, and annuities had gotten her to thinking what her mom and dad would do after one of them died.

> *They're doing great now and they love each other's company dearly, but what will life be like after one of them dies? I don't want the survivor to die of loneliness!*

Lisa wanted to be proactive so she had done some research and found a retirement community called Peaceful Place that seemed perfect for one of them to move into after the other one died.

Peaceful Place was founded more than 100 years ago as a home for retired Christian missionaries. The noble idea was that they would have a quiet place to live after their missionary work was done, and be surrounded by like-minded people. In return, they agreed that any money or investments they had would be turned over to Peaceful Place when they died.

Over time, it became evident that most missionaries had effectively taken a vow of poverty, which meant that Peaceful Place could not sustain itself without opening its homes to people who were not penniless. So, Peaceful Place began welcoming people who could and would pay to live in a community full of people with good moral principles.

Lisa explained that today Peaceful Place is a small community of about 300 people who believe in peace, social justice, and sustainability—just like her parents. In fact, people who apply to live in Peaceful Place must be at least 60 years old and submit a written personal statement attesting to their beliefs in peace, social justice, and sustainability. They also have to list ways in which they have contributed to these causes either through their jobs or volunteer work. It sounded daunting, but Lisa said it was no problem for her parents!

Each person (or couple) living in Peaceful Place has their own detached house, ranging from 600 to 1,800 square feet, so they have more independence and privacy than if they were living in an institutional building with adjoining apartments.

Lisa began reciting what appealed to her:

Even though they live in separate houses, there are lots of group activities such as morning stretching and afternoon art classes. There is a dining hall for people to eat together when they don't feel like cooking. They even have a community auditorium where they perform plays six times a year—mostly lively musicals such as Oklahoma, Singin' in the Rain, and Cabaret. They also rent buses to go to professional plays, concerts, and other events.

For outdoor activities, there are short hikes and bike rides almost every day. On Friday, there is an organized peace protest during the afternoon rush hour. They stand (or sit in wheelchairs) on a busy street corner waving signs such as "Love People, Not Guns" and "Great-Grandmothers for Peace."

Anyway, it sounds amazing and I'm thinking that, after one of my parents dies, the survivor can sell their house and use the proceeds to buy a home in Peaceful Place.

Jasmine said,

It does sound great. The only help I can give you is with the financials. What does it cost?

Lisa showed Jasmine a glossy pamphlet that had the expected smiling faces and glowing descriptions of the activities. The last page detailed the costs, which depend on the size of the home and whether it is for a single person or a couple. Lisa was thinking that a 1,000-square-foot, one-person home would be fine.

It turns out that there are two separate costs: a nonrefundable upfront fee plus monthly rent. For a one-person, 1,000-square-foot home, the upfront fee was currently $316,000 and the monthly rent was $3,500. The pamphlet said that both can be expected to increase every year.

Jasmine asked if the monthly rent covered utilities such as gas, electricity, television, and telephone. The answer was *no*. Jasmine asked what happens to the home after Lisa's surviving parent dies. The answer was that it goes back to Peaceful Place and they find a new tenant.

Jasmine was surprised by that answer:

So, your parent pays $316,000 but does not actually own the home?

When Lisa sheepishly admitted, "I guess not." Jasmine said,

That's surprising, for two reasons. First, $316,000 seems like a lot of money for not even getting to own the home. There are other small homes around here that don't cost much more than that—and the buyer owns the home and can either sell it or bequeath it. The people moving into Peaceful Place are already pretty old and, if they die soon after moving in, that's a lot of money paid for very little.

Second, remember how I told you that the British government once sold annuities for prices that didn't depend on how old the buyers were? They were a hot deal for young people and mainly bought by young people.

The same weird thing is going on here. The $316,000 price is the same for all ages even though older people are likely to die sooner. Also, the price is the same for men and women even though women tend to outlive men.

Your parents are in their 60s now and are likely to be in their 80s when one of them dies. It sounds harsh, but the survivor is looking at 10, maybe 20 years at most, living in Peaceful Place. A monthly rent of $3,500, growing at maybe 3 percent a year, sounds reasonable, but when you add on the nonrefundable $316,000, the effective monthly rate is pretty unreasonable.

Lisa was silent for a few moments, then asked hopefully:

How unreasonable?

Jasmine said simply,

I'll have to run the numbers.

Lisa mulled things over as she picked boysenberries in the garden while Jasmine entered numbers in one of the many computer programs she had written. A half hour later, she called Lisa back indoors and they each grabbed a bottle of sparkling water to go with the boysenberries:

> *Okay, I made a little table. We're talking about payments made over 10 or more years, so we have to take the time value of money into account, specifically how much your parents could earn if they invested the $316,000 instead of paying it to Peaceful Place.*
>
> *I looked at both a 5 percent annual return and a 10 percent return. We don't know how long your surviving parent will live, so I ran the numbers for 10 to 30 years. If both your parents live into their 80s, as they are expected to, the 10-year and 20-year calculations are the most relevant.*

Jasmine explained that the "effective initial monthly rent" numbers in the table take into account the $316,000 plus the 5 or 10 percent return on this money, and assume that the rent grows at 3 percent a year:

> *This means, for example, that if your surviving parent lives another 20 years, he or she could use the money that would have been paid to Peaceful Place to rent a home outside Peaceful Place for $5,078 a month (with the rent growing at 3% a year). They could rent a really, really nice home in this area for $5,078. Or they could rent a more modest place and have tens of thousands of dollars left over.*
>
> *If they rent a house outside Peaceful Place with an initial rent of $4,000, they would have $568,000 after 10 years if they earn a 5 percent return and $963,000 if they earn 10 percent. I know that*

Effective initial monthly rent

Years to Live	5% Return	10% Return
10	$6,391	$7,099
20	$5,078	$5,866
30	$4,646	$5,509

you and your brother don't need the money, but that could be a nice bequest to a deserving charity.

I know there are many things that money cannot buy, but there surely are ways for your surviving parent to enjoy life without paying so much money to Peaceful Place. There are plenty of relatives nearby —including you and your brother! Also, Irvine has three senior centers with lots of activities including cooking, dancing, art, fitness, and games. Your mom or dad could join a gardening club, a bridge club, or a Mahjong club. They could even join the war protestors on Friday afternoon!

Lisa said,

There's no way I could have done these calculations! It makes total sense and I'm kicking myself for not thinking it through. My mom or dad would essentially be giving away $316,000, on top of paying $3,500 in monthly rent. The survivor is probably not going to live much more than another 10 years, and that means they are paying $316,000 for very little. I also should have recognized that $316,000 will increase a lot because of compound interest if they invest the money instead of giving it to Peaceful Place.

Overall, I think that keeping the home they have and spending time with me, my brother, and their other friends and relatives makes a lot more sense.

Who knows, they might even have great-grandchildren to amuse them.

CHAPTER 22

Fake Intelligence

Jasmine was flabbergasted one Sunday evening by a phone call from Michael asking to meet Monday morning at the same coffee shop where they had talked about buying and renting homes. She didn't ask why and Michael didn't volunteer.

When he showed up late as usual, Michael didn't waste time with pleasantries:

Jazz, you've been really good about spending time tutoring my sister but, seriously, what's the point? We now have ChatGPT and other AI systems that can answer any question we ask them. The answers aren't always perfect, but they are good enough and are getting better every day. In a few years, you and your theories will be as obsolete and useless as swords, sundials, and slide rules.

I know you are old school—suspicious of cryptocurrencies and probably clueless about AI—but, still, you're super smart. Shouldn't you change with the times?

Jasmine was annoyed but smiled patiently. She didn't know what Michael intended to achieve with his barbs, but she chose to take it as a teachable moment:

Oh Michael. Thank you for worrying about me, but I am actually very familiar with ChatGPT and other large language models (LLMs). They are called LLMs because they scrutinize incredibly large amounts of text, including everything in Wikipedia, looking for statistical patterns. After some additional fine-tuning by humans, they are able to generate astonishingly humanlike conversations.

You were probably blown away when you first tried ChatGPT. I know I was—and so were millions of other people.

However, it's like a magic act in that the performance is astonishing, but it is just an illusion. LLMs don't really understand what words mean and they know nothing about the real world, so they have absolutely no idea whether the conversations they generate make sense or are nonsense. I like to say that they are always confident but often wrong.

Have you asked ChatGPT or any other LLM any financial questions?

Michael said, "Not really. Actually, none at all."
Jasmine opened her laptop and said,

Let's try one. I'll start with ChatGPT and a home-buying question like we talked about when we met before.

She typed in this query:

I'm thinking about buying a new home. The house costs $1 million. I will put $250,000 down and borrow $750,000 with a 30-year interest-only loan with a 4 percent interest rate. The annual interest payments will be $30,000. I estimate that the annual expenses will be property taxes $10,000; insurance $1,000; and maintenance $1,000. Please help me calculate the first-year rate of return.

ChatGPT instantly generated a 284-word response. It was all in perfect English and sounded authoritative. Jasmine used her cursor to show the highlights:

The net operating income (NOI) will be $0 since you're not renting the property out.

The total expenses for the first year are: Total Expenses = Annual Interest Payments + Property Taxes + Insurance + Maintenance = $30,000 + $10,000 + $1,000 + $1,000 = $42,000.

The Total Investment = Down Payment = $250,000. Now, plug these values into the formula: First-Year Rate of Return = Total

Expenses/Total Investment = ($42,000/$250,000) × 100 = 16.8 percent.

Jasmine invited Michael to study ChatGPT's answer: "What do you think?" Michael frowned as he read through the response:

Well, that's a mistake, saying that there is no income. It should have counted the rent savings as income.

The total expenses and total investment seem okay, but I don't understand why the expenses are counted as income for the homebuyer. The expenses are what the homebuyer pays, not what they receive. There is actually a 16.8 percent loss, not a 16.8 percent profit—though the loss would have been smaller or might have been a profit if the program had included the rent savings.

Jasmine said, "See, you're smarter than ChatGPT. Let's try Microsoft's Copilot." Copilot's 187-word response used the same $42,000 figure for total expenses. It ignored the rent savings and counted the $30,000 first-year interest payments as the first-year income. Subtracting the $42,000 in expenses and dividing by the total expenses, it gave a first-year return of −28.6 percent:

(Total Income − Total Expenses)/Total Expenses = ($30,000 − $42,000/$42,000 = −0.286

Michael literally blinked in disbelief:

Damn, it's dumb! The interest payments are not income! And they should have divided by the down payment, not the expenses!

Jasmine was inwardly gloating but she spoke softly, "Again, you're smarter than the computer. Want to try Google's Gemini?" Michael said, "Sure," and they soon had its 279-word response. It was just as glib, but even more wrong than ChatGPT and Copilot. Michael looked at it and said, "Wow, they sure know how to give long answers. Now if they only knew how to give good answers." Gemini had done several nonsensical calculations and concluded that the homebuyer's first-year return was a nonsensical –530 *percent*.

Michael shook his head, "Jeez."

Jasmine said,

> *None of these LLMs understand that rent savings should be counted as income. None of them know the difference between income and expenses. Perhaps even more damning, Gemini's confident conclusion that the homebuyer's first-year return is negative 530 percent clearly shows that it does not understand what words mean and knows nothing about the real world. Any semialert human knows that the first-year return from buying a house is not negative 530 percent.*

Michael clinched his teeth and nodded in reluctant agreement. Jasmine was sympathetic, but she persisted:

> *I could go on all day with examples of LLMs giving bad financial advice. And that's not going to change anytime soon. A lot of very smart people have been working very hard trying to figure out a way for computers to understand words and how they relate to the real world. They are not even close to an answer, in part because we know so little about how human brains do all the incredible things they do.*
>
> *You and I can do logical reasoning. We can make persuasive arguments. We can understand how some things cause other things to happen. We can identify obviously nutty claims. AI systems can't. They are fake intelligence.*

Michael said, "Okay, okay, you made your point. No need to gloat." Then, he said he had to leave for a house-showing and sprinted out the door.

CHAPTER 23

Turning a Page

Lisa's next visit to Jasmine was a big one with important news. She bounced inside with a huge smile and eager to make her big announcement:

I've mulled it over for quite some time now and I realize that I do like sales if—and it is a very important if—I believe in what I'm selling.

Aha! Jasmine knew that Lisa had made her big job decision. She let her continue:

There have been a lot of problems, though, with my current job. One, I don't like dressing up in expensive power clothes. That's not who I am.

Hmm. Now, Jasmine didn't know where this was headed. Lisa likes sales, but she doesn't like dressing up to make sales. Lisa certainly seemed happy—verging on deliriously happy—so she must have figured a way out of this dilemma. Lisa went on and Jasmine became increasingly curious and confused:

Two, I hate traveling, rushing to and from airports, hoping I won't be late and dreading waiting for my plane if I'm early. I don't like sitting next to strangers on planes who won't stop talking and may be spreading germs. It is especially awful for women traveling alone who have to listen to and rub shoulders with guys who are thinking this might be their lucky day.

Jasmine injected a strong amen:

True enough. That's why I wear baggy clothes and a fake wedding ring.

Lisa continued:

Three, I hate living out of hotels. I love sleeping in my own bed, sitting on my own sofa, cooking in my own kitchen, and doing everything else that makes my home my home.

Jasmine thought to herself, "Wow! This is a much longer list of complaints than I expected," but Lisa had even more.

Four, I hate the stress of having so much of my pay based on commissions. I understand that the company wants to incentivize its sales staff and weed out people who can't close deals and might even be undermining the company's reputation, but I've proven that I'm not a loser or a slacker. I deserve to be treated with respect and that means a stable salary that reflects my consistent value to the company.

Jasmine said,

Go girl! You should say all this to your bosses.

Lisa smirked,

I already have.... Meet the sales manager of our new cybersecurity division!
    Cyberattacks are real, growing, and incredibly expensive. We're building a terrific team of cybersecurity engineers and I am going to hire and manage the people who will sell the great products they create.
    We will be doing good things, protecting people from attacks by malicious governments, organized crime, and assorted sociopaths.
    This is something I really believe in and I can sell without feeling guilty. I can wear whatever I want (within reason). I don't have to travel (much). I can sleep (almost) every night in my own home. I

will be paid a huge salary (more money than I really need) plus a bonus if my team does exceptionally well.

Jasmine snuck in a "Congratulations" before Lisa finished her big announcement:

This is exactly what we were talking about—I love my new job so much it isn't really work. I actually wake up in the morning looking forward to "working." I'm not saying that I would do it for free, but I would be tempted.

Jasmine said, "Terrific! I think we need to celebrate," but Lisa sassed back:

Sorry. I just stopped by to share my good news. I need to go now because I'm so excited about getting to work.

CHAPTER 24

The Crossover

The next time that Lisa came to Jasmine's home, she apologized for rushing off after her big news:

Sorry about last time. I just wanted to tell you that I have a new job and I love it! Leaving so abruptly was just my impulsive way of showing you how crazy I am about it. It is truly like falling in love.

If you are ready to teach me more things, I am more than ready to learn.

Jasmine said that,

Finding a job you love is huge! I wasn't insulted. I was super-happy to see you super-happy. It made my day.

Let's talk today about another life-changing decision you can make. The key is to recognize how a commitment to saving money can change your life. We've already talked about the power of compound interest. I want to convince you that there is a huge payoff to spending less on stuff you don't need and, instead, building up your wealth by saving money you don't spend.

Jasmine pulled some tables and graphs out of a folder labeled "Crossover" and said,

Don't be intimidated. These are easy to understand and the payoff from understanding them is enormous.

She laughed and continued:

A lot of people (I'm not saying you), but a lot of people feel sorry for themselves and spend money on all sorts of junk trying to cheer

themselves up—retail therapy. Other people (and I'm not saying you), but a lot of people spend money in order to show others that they have money.

A great economist named Thorstein Veblen coined the term "conspicuous consumption" to describe people who spend inordinate amounts in order to impress other people: my house is bigger than your house; I have more cars than you do; my clothes cost more than your clothes.

I'm not accusing you of spending money in the past for retail therapy or conspicuous consumption. It doesn't matter what you did in the past since the past is past, but I'm asking you not to do it in the future.

I do know that, in the past, you spent a lot of money crafting an image that helped you close deals. That money wasn't wasted, but now that you are the sales manager, you can spend less and save more.

Lisa agreed:

Clearly, Erik and I spent too much. The evidence is undeniable. First, we had a house filled to the brim with crap. Second, I earned millions of dollars and we had almost no savings. I have no idea where the money went, but it went somewhere.

Jasmine said,

Don't beat yourself up or try to apportion blame between you and Erik. We can't change the past, but we can choose a future.

I want to show you a remarkable thing called the "crossover point." If you save and invest wisely, you will soon have so much wealth that you will be earning more income from your wealth than from your job.

Lisa was skeptical but Jasmine was confident she could convince her:

Suppose you are earning a nice round $320,000 a year after income taxes and spousal support and you save a quarter of that, $80,000. Do you think you could live comfortably spending $240,000 a year, or $20,000 a month?

Lisa nodded,

Sure. My mortgage payments are only $2,500 a month. Add in a couple thousand more for property taxes, insurance, and utilities and I would have plenty of money left over for food, clothes, entertainment, whatever. Spending $20,000 a month is almost embarrassing. I'm pretty sure I could save even more than $80,000 a year.

Jasmine interrupted,

Hold on soldier! We want to start with an easy goal. I don't want you feeling that you are scrimping and doing without.

Lisa laughed,

I won't be starving if I'm spending $20,000 a month!

Jasmine laughed, too,

Okay, so here's what I want you to do: $80,000 divided by 12 is $6,667. So every month, when you get paid, I want you to immediately put $6,667 into a mutual fund or brokerage account for investing. That way, you won't be tempted to spend more and save less than you promised yourself.

Lisa blurted out, "Can do!," and then Jasmine pulled out a graph.

I want to show you what is going to happen to your savings year after year.

    I assumed that your annual income grows by 3 percent a year and that you stick to your 25 percent saving rule. I also assumed that you earn an average of 10 percent a year on your savings, which has been the long-run average return from stocks. We can make other assumptions, but we will start with these.

Jasmine showed Lisa the figure below.

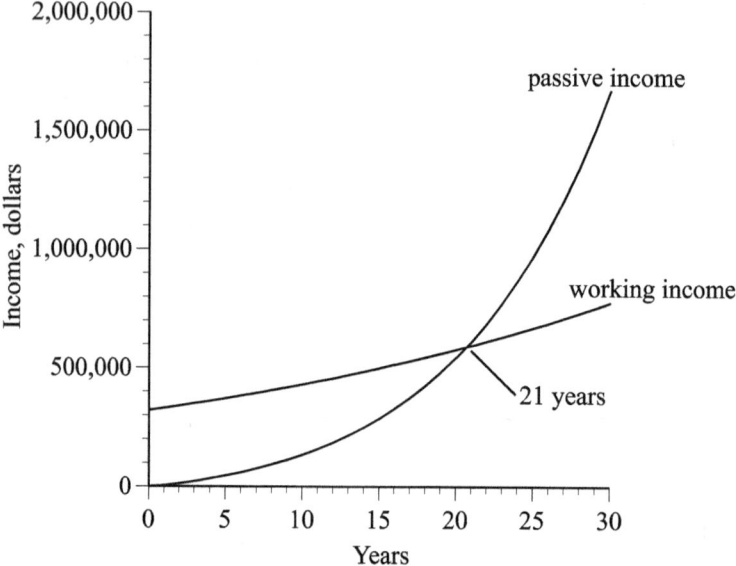

The "working income" line is the after-tax, after-alimony income from your job. It's initially $320,000 and grows by 3 percent a year. The "passive income" line is the income generated by your accumulated savings. It starts out at zero but, after 21 years, it will have caught up with your working income—both will be about $600,000 a year. Believe it or not, the savings that you have invested and reinvested will have grown to $6 million and be generating $600,000 a year in dividends and capital gains.

After that 21-year crossover point, your passive income will sprint past your working income. Thirty years from now, if you are still working, your annual passive income will be twice your working income—$1.6 million versus $800,000.

The good news is even better than this. To maintain your lifestyle, you don't need your passive income to replace your entire *working income, just the amount you spend each year. If you are saving 25 percent of your income and spending 75 percent, you only need your passive income to replace 75 percent of your working income. This figure shows that the spending crossover will happen in 18 years.*

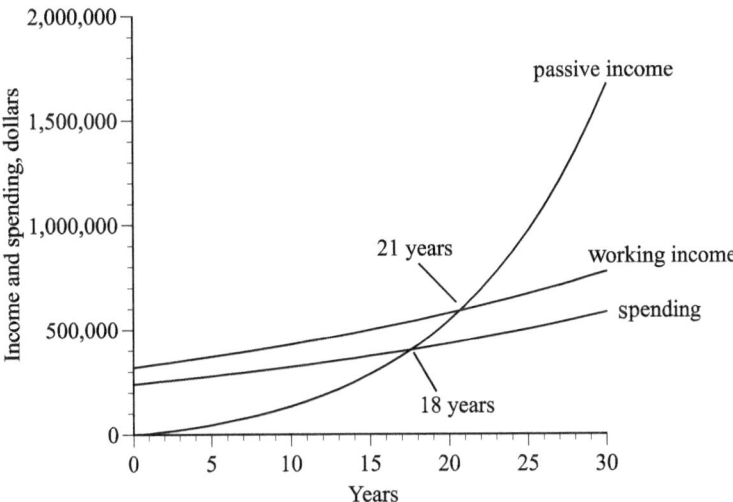

Lisa's scrunched-up face revealed her skepticism:

Are you sure? Did you check the math?

Jasmine laughed,

Oh yes. I've done these types of calculations many, many times. It doesn't really matter how much income a person makes. If they save a quarter of their income, which is growing at 3 percent a year, and invest their savings at 10 percent, the income crossover is always at 21 years and the spending crossover is always at 18 years.

Lisa made a "Wow" face and said it out loud:

Wow! So I can retire in 18 years and have enough wealth so that the income from my wealth will be enough to maintain my lifestyle?

Jasmine said,

The news is even better than that.

- *First, I ignored any money that your employer is putting into a retirement account for you.*
- *Second, I also ignored Social Security benefits.*
- *Third, you may well love your new job so much that you never want to retire. You can give your wealth away to your children or a favorite charity.*
- *Fourth, after 18 years, you will have a $4 million stock portfolio generating, on average, more than $400,000 a year in dividends and capital gains forever! You are not going to live forever, so you can actually spend more than $400,000 a year by gradually liquidating your stock portfolio.*

Lisa looked stunned:

This really is a life-changing eye-opener! I had no idea that the payoff from saving and investing could be so tremendous!

I do have one question, though. The stock market scares me. What if I don't buy stocks or I do buy stocks and they don't average 10 percent a year?

Jasmine said,

The rate of return you earn on your investments makes a difference, a big difference, because of the power of compound interest. If you only earn, say, 5 percent a year, the spending crossover is in 41 years instead of 18 years. That's why it is important to invest wisely in stocks, real estate, and other assets. You shouldn't be afraid of stocks, but that's a conversation for another time.

Lisa gave Jasmine a big hug and left smiling, eager to get to the job she loves, but thinking and rethinking about crossover points.

CHAPTER 25

Sadly Ungrateful

Lisa's already fragile relationship with her son, Noah, and her daughter, Anna, was pretty much destroyed by the divorce. The kids had spent most of their time growing up with Erik and they blamed Lisa for the divorce and for almost everything else that made them unhappy. Lisa suspected that Erik had planted and nurtured their anger but there wasn't much she could do about it. Arguing with them about Erik was only likely to push them further away.

Plus, Lisa was not particularly sympathetic to many of the choices her children had made. She was frustrated and regretted that she had not helped them make better decisions.

Noah was a wannabe artistic type. He wanted to go to Hollywood and make films that told stories about important things, such as war and poverty. Not that no one had ever made films about war and poverty. Not that Noah knew anything about war and poverty. He had never been in the military, let alone a war, and he had never been poor. Nor was he particularly good at filmmaking. When he showed his family the short movies that he made in his high school film classes, they reminded Lisa of nothing more than homemade family vacation videos.

It was hardly surprising that Hollywood wasn't much interested and that Noah wanted his mom and dad to finance his filmmaking. Mom told Noah that he should go to college and get a real job. Dad told Noah that a lot of geniuses never went to college and wrote him a big check. No wonder Noah liked dad more!

Anna was a different story. She couldn't wait to go to college, not because she wanted to prepare for a job but because she wanted to party hearty. Anna had always been popular. She was beautiful—no question about it—and she knew how to dress and act like a party girl, and that's what she had become by the time she headed off to college—USC, because of its party-school reputation. The sororities fought over her and she chose Kappa Kappa Gamma, which is famous (or infamous, depending on how you look at it) for being very selective and chock-full of dumb, blonde cuties. No ugly girls allowed!

Being in LA, there were lots of concerts, shows, and such to go to when Anna wasn't hanging around the Kappa Kappa Gamma sorority house or at a frat party, and Erik gave her enough money to do whatever she wanted. Classes were not a priority. Choose the easiest ones and do the bare minimum to pass—which isn't much these days.

Colleges don't want students dropping out. It hurts their bottom line and the *U.S. News* rankings—both of which affect the top administrators' already bloated salaries. So, the admins do their best to make colleges fun and keep students happy. Nowadays, colleges even serve real food in the dining halls. This need-to-please attitude is also one reason for the rampant grade inflation. It used to be that average students got C grades. Now, average students at private colleges like USC get A grades because, if they didn't, the students might be sad or angry.

A student who gets a B+ may complain bitterly to the professor: "I can't get a job with a B+ grade." If the professor refuses to up the grade, the unhappy student can go the Dean of Students and complain about how traumatizing it is to get a B+. The professor is summoned to the dean's office and asked if there isn't "something" that can be done. Most professors get the message, especially if they don't have tenure and depend on student course evaluations to keep their jobs. The B+ magically turns into an A.

The easiest way to avoid the hassle is to give every student an A grade right off the bat. No complaining. No trips to the Dean's office. No magical grade adjustments. Problem solved.

One well-meaning professor tells his students at the start of each term that he uses "labor-based grading," which means that grades are based on effort rather than mastery. In practice, he gives A grades to every student who comes to most of his classes because showing up for class demonstrates real effort these days.

Lisa was disappointed with both her children. Neither of them worked as hard as she did when she was their age. Neither went to

Harvard. Neither was likely to land a high-paying job. Both were likely to be dependent on Lisa's income—funneled through Erik—for the rest of their lives. The only alternative she could see was for Anna to get an Mrs. degree by marrying a rich USC frat boy.

Lisa was even more upset with her ex, Erik, who she blamed for the rocky paths they were on. They didn't know the value of hard work. They didn't know how to deal with disappointment. They had zero resilience. They hadn't learned these life lessons at home and they weren't going to learn them by making bad films and going to a make-everybody-happy college.

Still, maybe it wasn't too late. Now that Lisa had gotten her life under control, she was hopeful that this might be the time to repair her relationship with her children (and maybe, just maybe, Erik).

It did not go well.

Lisa telephoned Anna first because she was not as disappointed with Anna as she was with Noah. At least Anna was going to college, even if she was trying as hard as she could to avoid anything remotely academic.

Anna answered after nine rings with a wary, "Hi, mom." Lisa ignored the snarkiness:

Hi, honey. I was just calling to see how you are doing.

Anna waited several seconds as if she expected Lisa to say more. Finally, Anna broke the silence:

Mom, you almost never call and you never much cared how I was doing. What's wrong? Did you lose your job? Are you getting married again? Frankly, I don't think you're cut out to be a wife, let alone a mother.

Ouch! That was a full-on body blow. Anna must really hate her. Still, Lisa tried to be civil and maybe even friendly:

No, I didn't lose my job. In fact, I got promoted to a better job where I won't have to work such long hours and travel so much. I really am just calling to see how you are doing. Anna, I care about you.

Anna again waited several seconds, this time choosing her words carefully:

It's a little late for that. Maybe you shouldn't have worked so much and been gone so much when you were married and Noah and I were living at home.... Mom, I don't think you cared about me or Noah or Dad. You just cared about your stupid job.
  Listen, I gotta go.

Lisa couldn't hold it any longer:

No, you listen. Who do you think paid for everything you've ever had, including your happy-times college? It certainly wasn't Erik and it certainly wasn't you.

Anna hung up.

Lisa had even meaner thoughts but she had swallowed them. She remembered a wonderful psychology professor at Harvard who had talked one time about the damaging physical and mental consequences on repressing anger. But the professor also warned the class that, "Once the toothpaste is out of the tube, it's very hard to put it back in." The fallout from saying hurtful things in anger can be far worse than the strain from keeping your mouth shut. The hard-but-obvious solution is to find a way to let off steam without permanently damaging relationships. Walloping tennis balls and punching a boxing bag is a start. So is an occasional scream. Even better is to feel empathy for people who irritate you. Yeah, they're annoying but there's probably a reason why they are the way they are. Sympathy is more appropriate than contempt.

  Lisa was frustrated and sad. She had tried to reestablish a connection with her daughter but Anna wasn't interested. Maybe she would have better luck with Noah.
  Nope.

Lisa sent Noah a text message, proposing that they meet outside a local coffee shop. After several delays and evasive responses, Noah finally agreed to a Sunday morning meeting.

Lisa got there early, fearful that Noah would bolt if she wasn't on time. It was Noah who was late, 40 minutes late. Maybe he was dissing her. Maybe he hoped she would give up and leave. Either way, he finally did show and Lisa was determined to be on her best behavior. She got up and tried to give Noah a hug but he was as cold as a wax sculpture at Madame Tussauds.

She tried kind words instead:

Hi, honey. I wanted to meet to see how you are doing.

Noah continued doing his imitation of a wax sculpture. In a lifeless voice, he answered,

I'm fine.

Lisa didn't give up:

Tell me about your latest film project.

The wax sculpture didn't give up either:

Dad's paying for it because he believes in me. I hope to have it finished next year.

Lisa couldn't resist:

You do know where your father is getting that money, right?

Then she backtracked:

I'm sorry. I didn't mean to say that. What's your film about?

The wax sculpture didn't seem to care about the dig or the apology:

My film is about how hard it is to be poor in this capitalist train wreck of a country.

That was too much for Lisa:

Noah, you have never, ever been poor. And do you know why? Because we live in a country where I have worked hard all my life and have been paid enough to give you a nice home with nice clothes, good food, and all the games and toys you could ever want. I paid for your Audi and I am paying for your film—because we live in a country that recognizes and rewards my hard work.

She wanted to say, "You're as clueless as your sister," but she remembered toothpaste erupting from a tube and kept that angry thought to herself. The wax sculpture got up and waddled away from the table without saying goodbye. Lisa shook her head sadly: "That boy needs to lose some weight! What in the heck does he know about being poor?"

There seemed to be no point in trying to make peace with Erik-the-ex, and Lisa didn't bother trying.

CHAPTER 26

Control the Small Stuff

Lisa showed up at Jasmine's house the following Tuesday, saddened and frustrated that her children spent so much money without ever pausing to say, "Thank you." Jasmine decided that this might be a good time to talk about ways that people can reduce their spending and increase their savings:

Pretty much everybody buys things they don't really need to buy. Sometimes it's an addiction, such as smoking and gambling. Sometimes it's for comfort. Sometimes it's because we aren't paying attention.

You and I may not waste as much as Anna and Noah, but we do waste a bit. Some casual spending might seem so small and inconsequential that it doesn't matter one way or another, but small things can add up to big things.

Lisa made a quizzical face and said, "Tell me more." Jasmine was happy to:

I have an eye-opening exercise that I do with many of my clients. I ask them to look at their checking-account and credit-card statements for the past 12 months and put the transactions into three categories:

Housing-related: Either the rent they pay or, if they own their homes, the mortgage payments, property taxes, insurance, utilities, and so on.
Personal: Food, clothing, entertainment, and everything else.
Savings: Money transferred to a mutual fund, brokerage account, or something similar.

Jasmine then showed Lisa this worksheet:

	Spending/Saving Worksheet Over the Past 12 Months	
1	Average monthly before-tax pay	$_____
2	Average monthly take-home pay + retirement contributions	$_____
3	Average monthly house-related spending	$_____
4	Average monthly other spending	$_____
5	Average monthly saving including retirement contributions	$_____
6	Percent house-related spending: 100*(3)/(2)	_____%
7	Percent other spending: 100*(4)/(2)	_____%
8	Percent total spending: (6) + (7)	_____%
9	Percent saving: 100*(5)/(2)	_____%

Jasmine added a caution:

Most housing expenses can be identified by checks or direct withdrawals from a checking account, but there may be a few expenses that are paid by credit card and then lumped together in a credit card bill that is paid out of a checking account. Another important complication is that you should count money that you and/or your employer put into a retirement account as savings. You can find these numbers on your monthly pay stub.

After Lisa studied the worksheet for a few moments, Jasmine said,

I then ask my clients to compare their answers to (8) and (9) to an 80–20 rule of thumb: 80 percent spending, 20 percent saving. Ideally, I would like them to save 25 percent and that's the number we used in our crossover calculations a few weeks ago, but most people are so far from 25 percent that it is a real accomplishment to get to 20 percent. If 20 percent is too daunting, we settle for a temporary 90–10 rule. Once they see that 10 percent savings is doable, we can aim higher.

Another rule of thumb is that a homeowner's housing cost (mortgage payment, property taxes, and home insurance—but not counting utilities) should not be more than 40 percent of take-home

pay. There is some flexibility here but, if housing-related spending is more than 50 percent of take-home pay, there is usually a financial squeeze that makes saving difficult.

These guidelines can help us see whether our spending is excessive. It sounds boring, but can be very empowering.

Jasmine explained:

When someone is nowhere near the 80–20 rule, we dig deeper for reasons. They might be shocked, for example, to discover how much they spend going to restaurants or having food delivered to their home.

Jasmine then suggested that,

Another way to approach the goal of getting to the 80–20 goal is to prioritize different categories of spending; for example, making a list from top priority to lowest priority.

Together, they shuffled and reshuffled items until they came up with this list:

1. Groceries
2. Transportation
3. Health care
4. Childcare
5. Internet and cell phone
6. Clothing
7. Fitness
8. Streaming services
9. Dining out
10. Personal beauty care
11. Entertainment
12. Vacation and travel
13. Furniture and home decor
14. Hobbies

Jasmine then said,

I'm not saying that you have to eliminate hobbies or stop buying furniture. I am saying that it can be helpful to think about which things are more important and which are less so.

I've also found that most people are really surprised by how seemingly small expenses, done over and over, really add up.

Lisa said, "Such as?" and Jasmine was happy to answer her question:

A favorite example for financial planners is a daily trip to a local coffee shop. A coffee shop can be a convenient, neutral place to meet someone for business or pleasure, but a habit of getting caffeine doses at coffee shops every day or several times a day can be an expensive habit.

Maybe you spend $10 on a coffee and pastry and think, "It's only $10; I can certainly afford it." That may be true, but spending $10 day after day, instead of investing that $10, can add up to serious money. Let me do some quick calculations.

Jasmine went over to her desk and punched some numbers into her computer.

These are just examples, but they give the general picture. Suppose you are currently spending $10 a day on coffee and pastries and this habitual spending will grow by 3 percent each year. If you instead save this money and invest in stocks earning, on average, a 10 percent return, guess how much you will have after 20 years?

Lisa plucked a number out of the air and shrugged her shoulders: "$10,000?" Jasmine laughed,

Not even close! You will have $270,193 after 20 years and $824,743 after 30 years.

Now it was Lisa who laughed,

You know what that is? It's "a penny saved is a penny earned" on steroids because of the power of compounding.

Jasmine said,

*You're right about the compounding, but it is actually a penny saved, **two** pennies earned. With federal and California taxes, you're in roughly a 50 percent tax bracket. This means you have to earn two pennies in order to save one penny. Saving $10 on coffee and pastries is like earning $20 from your job. Think about this two-to-one ratio every time you are tempted to buy something you can do without.*

Plus, it's probably better to cut back on the pastries. As for coffee, I'm not going to ask you to give that up. In fact, there is a lot of evidence that coffee is actually good for your health. But I do want you to think about something: You know the coffee I serve you here?

Lisa said, "Sure, that's great coffee." Jasmine then revealed that she made the coffee with a De'Longhi Magnifica that she bought in 2003 for a few hundred dollars. More than 20 years later, it is still pumping out great coffee:

Making coffee at home is not only much less expensive, but saves you the time and energy it takes to go to a coffee shop. It also gives you a chance to try different coffee beans. Just make sure you buy whole beans and have a coffee machine that has a built-in grinder.

There are well-known coffee-bean brands such as Lavazza and Illy and lesser-knowns such as Stumptown, Stone Street, and Blue Bottle. You can also experiment with wonderful coffee beans with great names, such as Kicking Horse Kick Ass and Death Wish.

Lisa laughed, "Those last two sound irresistible!"

Jasmine then said,

There are lots of things like this—coffee and pastries at a coffee shop—little indulgences that, done over and over, end up being pretty expensive.

She was on a roll and she kept rolling:

Another one of my pet peeves is gardeners who are paid $50 a week or more to make a brief appearance, mow and blow, and skedaddle. If people fired their gardeners, they could invest $200/month or more (growing at 3% a year) at a 10 percent annual return, and they would have $180,129 after 20 years and $549,829 after 30 years.

Plus, as Uncle Andrew said, "Exercise is medicine." It's good for the body and soul to go outdoors, appreciate nature, get your hands dirty, and push around a manual lawnmower. A well-built, four-blade push mower can be bought for less than $100 and most people already own a rake and broom. They just need to use them.

Lisa nodded her agreement, and Jasmine pushed on:

Another example is gym memberships. People get the well-intentioned idea that they should exercise regularly. I agree completely with their intentions, but good intentions are hardly enough.

They sign up at a local gym and, "for convenience," arrange to have the monthly fee automatically charged to a credit card. After a few visits, their willpower wanes as there always seems to be something else to do that is more important or more fun than going to the gym. Soon, they are not going at all while their credit card continues being charged, month-after-month, for a membership they don't use.

This is a bonanza for gyms. They get regular income without long lines at the machines, but it is a money pit for their no-show customers.

Lisa raised her hand, "Guilty!" Jasmine laughed and continued,

I'm not saying that exercise is bad. Exercise is terrifically healthy and invigorating. After a 20-mile bike ride, I feel virtuous and exhilarated. I am saying that unused gym memberships are a waste of money. Go for a walk. Ride a bike. If you want to use a rowing

machine or weights, then buy them, put them in your garage, and use them.

Lisa said, "Sold!" and Jasmine took a slight detour:

Remember when you told me how cheap your parents were when you were growing up?

Lisa nodded, "Yep."

They weren't being cheap. They were making choices. They didn't have a lot of money and they decided that it was better for you and Michael to live in a house near your relatives and near great public schools than to drink soda pop in restaurants and eat popcorn in movie theaters. They decided that it was better for you to go to tennis lessons than to go to a barber shop. They decided that it was better to .... Well, I'm sure you get the point.

Lisa's eyes widened and she muttered, "You're right! I think I need to say thank you."

Then Jasmine added a warning:

On the other hand, sometimes people are truly cheap in ways that turn out to be expensive, as in the old proverb "penny wise but pound foolish." For example, a chef who buys a cheap knife that cuts poorly; a gardener who buys cheap pruning shears that break quickly; a cyclist who buys a cheap bicycle that is not safe to ride. This is also true of services. Some dentists, for example, seem inexpensive, but then try to upsell patients on expensive procedures they don't need.

Important medical procedures are another good example. I used to play pickup co-ed soccer games and, one day, a new guy showed up who ran with a crazy limp. I asked him if he was okay and he said, "Yeah, fine." He explained that he had broken his shinbone playing soccer a few years earlier and, not having medical insurance, he had the bone set by a friend of his who was a veterinarian—and evidently not a very good one.

After Lisa stopped laughing, Jasmine said,

Here is a story with a happier ending. My father had knee replacement surgery when he was 71. The doctor who was assigned to him was relatively inexperienced and told my dad that he would have to cut muscles, tendons, and ligaments to get to the knee joint and that there would be a long and painful recovery, after which my dad's future would be spent mostly sitting on a couch watching television.

Fortunately, one of my dad's friends had gone out of network to have his knee-replacement surgery done by an extremely competent surgeon who routinely uses a minimally invasive procedure. My dad got Medicare to pay for his surgery, but it would have been worth it to pay out of pocket for a high-quality surgeon. Now he's almost as active as he was 20 years ago.

Not that you are about to have your knees replaced but, when it comes to medical care, it seldom pays to be cheap.

Jasmine wrapped it up:

I've been on this soap box way too long. I'll just say a few more words and then shut up. I'm no saint. We can all surely think of many small purchases that we can do without: drinking in bars, eating at restaurants, having food delivered to our homes, watching movies in theaters. These are all fine as once-in-a-while treats but, done regularly, they can be pretty expensive. Nor do we need to fill our homes with redundant clothes, questionable art, and expensive dust-catchers.

Lisa interrupted,

No, no, no. Don't apologize. I've learned a lot and I like it when you get excited and jump on your soap box. I just wish we had time to talk about cars, jewelry, vacation homes, and other big-ticket items.

Jasmine said, "I promise, next time we will—and, you're right, there is a lot more to talk about."

Lisa then left to buy a coffee machine and some Kick Ass coffee.

CHAPTER 27

Control the Big Stuff

Jasmine started their next meeting with a question:

Do you remember when we talked about conspicuous consumption a few weeks ago? It is generally considered bad manners to brag about how much income or wealth we have, so a lot of people instead advertise their prosperity by buying things that most people can't afford: "My car is more expensive than your car because I can afford to buy my car and you can't."

This naturally leads to conspicuous-consumption competitions where the participants keep trying to outspend each other. The only people guaranteed to be happy are the merchants peddling high-priced crap.

Jasmine said that she had far too many examples but she wanted to start with vacation homes. Only about 6 percent of Americans own vacation homes so having one will impress most people—especially if the home is somewhere fancy that people have heard of, like Hawaii or Aspen.

She acknowledged that vacation homes can be wonderful and are sometimes worth the cost. Jasmine's parents were both professors at Cornell in upstate New York for many years and they owned a three-bedroom, three-bath home on Spitfire Lake, which is a 4-to-5 hour drive northeast of Cornell, just an hour or so from the Canadian border. The house is on 8 acres, with 750 feet of lake frontage, and built from one of those log-cabin kits where you pick a design and the company ships you the wood for the walls and roof, along with windows, doors, and everything else you need—all precut so that you can put it together like a giant Ikea project.

> *Just joking! No way were my professor parents going to assemble that beast. They paid a local contractor to hire a competent crew and do the job.*
>
> *Every summer, as soon as school was out, we headed to our cabin, where we stayed for 3 months or so, until school started up in the fall. Spitfire Lake is great for swimming, sailing, canoeing, kayaking, windsurfing, and so on. Lots of fish, too, though we weren't much into fishing. Too boring! I'd much rather windsurf for two hours than fish for two hours.*

Jasmine said that the great thing about owning their vacation home was that they could leave all their stuff there in the fall and it would be waiting for them when they returned the next year: clothes, pots and pans, a Sunfish sailing boat, canoes, kayaks, windsurfing boards, and so on. They could have rented a vacation home in a different place every summer but they wouldn't have had all the stuff that made their summers so much fun.

> *I also have to admit that it felt great to have this family ritual of going back to a familiar house on a familiar lake every year.*

Jasmine said that the financials for buying a vacation home are pretty much the same as the financials for buying any home to live in: make a list of the annual income and expenses and calculate the home dividend. One wrinkle with a vacation home is that it might be rented out part of the year so you should consider: (1) how much you would have had to pay to rent the home during the time you live in it plus (2) the income you get from renting it to others when you are not there. The tax rules are a bit complicated so best done by an expert or by using some reliable tax software.

A convincing analysis should also take into account uncertainties in the projections, just as they had done with solar panels. They might try different scenarios, making a variety of plausible assumptions about how fast rents will increase in the future, how often they will stay in the home, and how many days the home will be rented out.

Jasmine said that,

In my experience, vacation homes are usually just conspicuous consumption unless you stay for several months or can get really good rental income. It seldom makes financial sense to buy a house that you only live in for a few weeks a year and leave empty the rest of the time. Far better to give yourself the option of going to different places on your vacations and renting a place—even staying at a Four Seasons or Ritz-Carlton.

Ben Stein, economist, author, and television personality, owns around a dozen homes (the exact number fluctuates year to year). He says that it gives him great pleasure to open the front door of one of his many homes and say, "This is mine." Maybe so, but a craving for house-collecting is a pretty expensive addiction.

A similar big-ticket item is a camper, recreational vehicle (RV), or motor home—essentially a vacation home on wheels. Jasmine said that these give you the freedom to vacation all over the country and save you the cost of staying in motels and hotels but they can cost as much as a real home and, unlike real homes, they only last 10 to 20 years.

Jasmine asked Lisa if she had noticed the big RV parked in front of a house down the street. It has been parked there for more than a year now—it was little more than a display of conspicuous consumption. Buying an expensive motor home you hardly use is about as financially foolish as buying a vacation home you seldom use.

Jasmine said that

The financial analysis is pretty much the same as for a vacation home. Make a list of all the income and expenses. The income is essentially the money you save by not staying in hotels and motels. The ongoing annual expenses include insurance, campsite fees, gasoline, utilities, and maintenance. There will also be storage fees if you don't have a place to park it.

Lisa had trouble keeping track of everything and, when Jasmine noticed her dazed expression, she said:

It's probably easier if I show you a table of numbers. This is just a hypothetical example because the numbers depend so much on the model you buy and how often you use it. There are some lessons though.

Jasmine showed Lisa a table for a hypothetical nice-but-not-luxurious RV that cost $100,000 plus a 7.75 percent sales tax, making the total cost $107,750. Jasmine assumed that the owners would make four 7-day trips a year, drive a total of 10,000 miles, and, if they didn't have the RV, would pay $800 a night to stay at a very nice resort. Thinking on the margin, they compared driving the RV on their vacation trips with driving their Tesla.

Annual RV Dividend	
Hotel cost ($800/night)	$22,400
Registration fee and use tax	-$7,500
Insurance	-$1,500
Campsite fees ($100/night)	-$2,800
Gasoline	-$5,000
Utilities	-$3,000
Maintenance	-$2,500
RV dividend	$100

The bottom line is a minuscule $100 first-year RV dividend. The RV owners could certainly expect to get a better return if they invested their $107,750 in stocks and other financial assets. This is one of those cases, however, where it is important to look ahead. California's registration fee and use tax depend on the value of the vehicle, which declines over time. The difference between the hotel savings and the other RV expenses may go up or down over time. A third consideration is that

RVs don't last forever. The RV dividend will end when the RV goes kaput.

Taking all these things into account and making plausible assumptions as needed, the implied annual rate of return on the RV works out to be 3.9 percent if it lasts 20 years and negative 11 percent if it lasts only 10 years. Jasmine concluded:

> *As usual, I highly recommend doing the calculations with a variety of reasonable assumptions—like how often it will be used and what kind of hotels the owners would stay in if they didn't own an RV.*
>
> *I've done this for a few clients and, so far, it has always turned out that they would be better off staying in a motel or hotel—even a very expensive one—unless they plan to sell their house and live in a motor home year round, which is a pretty radical lifestyle change. How many people can throw away 90 percent or more of what they own?*

Jasmine then said that when she thought about RVs, she pictured a boat on wheels, and that boats (or even worse, yachts) are generally another big-ticket waste of money—essentially a hole in the water into which you throw money.

She told Lisa that one of her friends from Wharton (Herb) had gone to teach at Yale and that another professor there (Martin) had a sailboat that he seldom used. Herb asked if he could take the boat out one sunny Sunday and Martin was happy to say yes: "It's good that someone is getting some use out of it."

Herb sailed out of New Haven Harbor into Long Island Sound. He had to sail under a traffic bridge and did so easily because it was low tide. Coming back in the afternoon, he didn't notice that it was now high tide. The mast hit the bridge and broke, capsizing and sinking the boat. Fortunately, no one was injured but Herb was distraught.

After drying himself off and changing clothes, he went to Martin's house and apologized profusely until Martin put up his hand to stop him from carrying on:

Please stop the sad blathering. I have insurance and I feel like a tremendous weight has been lifted from my shoulders. All I want to do is thank you.

Jasmine said, "I think that tells you all you need to know about boats."

For over-the-top conscious consumption, New Haven Harbor is essentially nothing compared to Newport Harbor near where they live. There are nearly 10,000 yachts and mega-yachts docked in the harbor, worth, in total, several billion dollars. Most just sit there, day after day, to be admired by locals and tourists.

Jasmine then said that, since they had gone from vacation homes to RVs to yachts, it made sense to turn to expensive cars, another potential extravagance. She argued that there is no good reason to spend lavishly on cars other than to impress your neighbors and the drivers of the cars you zoom past on freeways.

For example, the Pacific Coast Highway, also known as PCH or CA1, hugs the California coast, giving spectacular views of the Pacific Ocean as it winds 650 miles from Dana Point in Southern California up to Northern California, where it intersects the 101, which continues north through Oregon and Washington, almost to the Canadian border.

PCH is often narrow with thrilling twists and turns that can make it feel like driving in a Grand Prix race, as Lisa knew all too well. Her daughter, Anna, had once taken a day off from high school and driven her cherry red Miata convertible up the PCH toward San Francisco. She had barely gotten past Los Angeles when she was arrested for driving 80 mph. Anna said the police were picking on her for driving a red convertible. Lisa said she was lucky she hadn't killed herself. Another one of many mother–daughter disagreements they had.

Jasmine laughed and said that there are stretches of the PCH in Newport Beach where people living in multimillion-dollar homes on both sides of the highway are continually annoyed by people driving Lamborghinis, Porsches, Ferraris, Aston Martins, McLarens, and other high-priced cars with loud exhaust systems. Most cars are designed to muffle the sound of exhaust gasses. Noise enthusiasts spend hundreds or thousands of dollars to reverse that and pump up the volume.

> *I've biked that highway and it can be pretty intimidating when a varooming car speeds by. The police have put up noise warning signs but they don't seem to have much effect.*
>
> *The frustrated homeowners probably should have thought of the noise pollution when they bought their homes! My point, though, is that the people driving these cars are showing off. They bought their fancy cars and modified the exhaust systems in order to draw attention to themselves, not because they wanted an economical way to get from one place to another.*

She showed Lisa a picture she had taken on her phone while biking along the PCH:

Jasmine then said that clothing and jewelry are other examples of wretched excess. She had a professor at Wharton who always wore expensive pinstripe power suits:

> *When he began a lecture, he would pull his left sleeve back, remove his gold Rolex watch, and put it on the table in front of him.*
>
> *There was no real reason why he had to dress like he was a Wall Street banker or why he had to wear, let alone take off, a Rolex. He just wanted the students to think that he was a very successful investor.*

Lisa giggled and shook her head:

> *I know all about dressing for success, trying to pass yourself off as more accomplished than you really are.*

Jasmine quickly responded:

> *Don't be embarrassed. Lots of people do it. On the other hand, lots of successful people let their successes speak for themselves.*
>
> *I had professors at Wharton who dressed in casual clothes—maybe even too casual—because they knew they were the smartest people in the room and the students would be wowed by their brains, no matter what they wore. They never used notes or slides and they could answer any question thrown at them. They were a lot more impressive than the poser in the pinstripe suit.*
>
> *One brilliant professor wore clothes that he bought at Goodwill. (He also patched the side of his F-150 by welding on some metal from a busted clothes washer.) I even had one professor—maybe the smartest of them all—who always wore t-shirts.*

She went on:

> *Seriously, who needs a Rolex watch, Gucci handbag, or diamond necklace? Who needs three Rolex watches, five Gucci handbags, and*

two dozen necklaces? Too many people make impulsive purchases of expensive jewelry and junk that they don't need and seldom wear.

Conspicuous consumption is fueled by peer pressure, which can be intense if you live in a place where people pay preposterous amounts for obscure brands of water and olive oil, and take weekend trips to Cabo, Aspen, and places that you and I have never heard of, let alone been to.

I'm sure you noticed all the Teslas and fancy German cars in Irvine. That's not a coincidence.

Lisa laughed,

Yeah, we had two white Teslas, a BMW, and an Audi.

Jasmine ended the meeting with positive encouragement:

Impulse spending is always hazardous but it is particularly dangerous when buying expensive things like a Lamborghini sports car, a Marchi motor home, or dressers full of overpriced clothes and jewelry.

Believe me, Lisa, you don't need any of that crap. People are going to love and respect you for who you are, not for what you buy.

CHAPTER 28

The Greater Fool Theory

At their next meeting, Lisa said that her job was going even better than she had expected or hoped. She had extremely competent colleagues who were fun to work with and she had a great sales staff that loved her. There was less stress and guilt about peddling things people don't really need. The company had terrific engineers who were creating great products—indeed, often unexpectedly great products. She was learning the wisdom of Steve Jobs' assertion that, "People don't know what they want until you show it to them." People certainly didn't know that they wanted iPhones.

She told Jasmine,

I'm not saying that we will create something as great as the iPhone, but you never know…

Lisa's spending had dropped precipitously and now she had a very welcome problem. She needed to decide how to invest all the money she was saving!

Jasmine began her advice by reminding Lisa of the Moon Festival discussion of Beanie Babies and cryptocurrencies:

As I said then, I like investments that generate income because, even if the price goes down, you are still getting a return on your investment. In fact, if the price goes down you might want to buy more.

Jasmine held up a piece of paper and said that she wanted to read Lisa a quotation from that legendary, sensible midwestern investor, Warren Buffett:

> *To refer to a personal taste of mine, I'm going to buy hamburgers the rest of my life. When hamburgers go down in price, we sing the 'Hallelujah Chorus' in the Buffett household. When hamburgers go up in price, we weep. For most people, it's the same with everything in life they will be buying—except stocks. When stocks go down and you can get more for your money, people don't like them anymore.*

Lisa nodded, "That's simple and profound." Jasmine laughed and said,

> *You should read his annual letters to Berkshire shareholders. They are full of plain-spoken, well-written wisdom.*
>
> *I want to add one more thing about income-producing investments. In not every case, but in most cases, the income from stocks, real estate, and so on grows with the overall economy. So, if stock prices or real estate prices drop, they won't stay depressed forever. As the income from stocks and real estate grows over time, they become more valuable and their prices will inevitably go up.*
>
> *How could it be otherwise? Suppose that an investment is yielding an income of $500 a year and has a market price of $10,000. That's a 5 percent return. If the income grows over time while the market price stays at $10,000, then the one-year return grows to 6 percent, 7 percent, and so on. At some point, the income will be so enticingly large that demand for this investment will increase and the market price will rise, too.*

Jasmine said that people like Warren Buffett who are attracted to investments that yield substantial income relative to their price are called "value investors." They are not interested in speculative gambles that yield no income. They leave those to the Greater Fools who pay a foolish price because they hope to find even greater fools who will pay an even more foolish price.

It is the Greater Fools who power speculative bubbles, buying as prices rise because they think prices will keep rising. Their delusional purchases push prices up until the foolish buyers are outnumbered by people who want to cash in their gains by selling. Once prices stop rising and start falling, prices collapse because there is no good reason to buy something that yields no income and has a falling price.

During the Dutch Tulip mania bubble, a tulip bulb that cost $25 (in 2024 dollars) in the summer of 1636 traded for $200 in January 1637 and $2,500 a few weeks later. Then prices collapsed. Jasmine showed Lisa a graph of an index of tulip bulb prices.

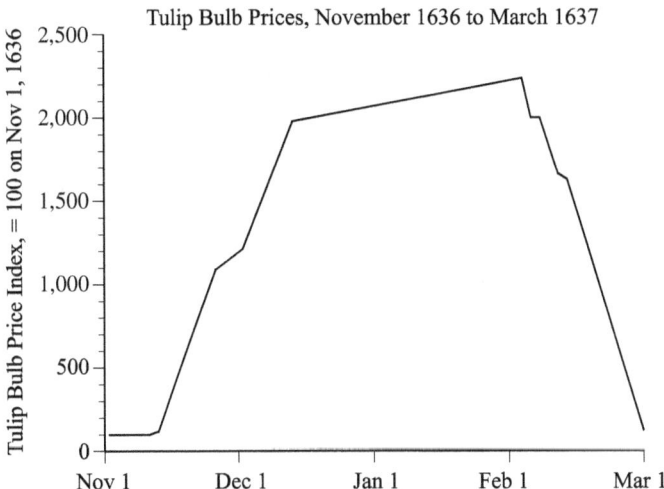

Tulip Bulb Prices, November 1636 to March 1637

Another bubble—the South Sea Bubble—involved a British company called the South Sea Company. It was founded in 1711 and had been granted exclusive trading rights in South America by the British government. These rights were essentially worthless because Spain and Portugal controlled most of South America.

The South Sea Company had no plausible prospects of making any profits, but it raised cash by selling more stock and it propped up its stock price by lending money to people who bought shares at ever higher prices. In 1720, the company audaciously agreed to take over Britain's national debt even though it had no plausible way of paying the interest due on the debt other than by selling more stock.

The company's stock price soared from £129 on January 29, 1720, to £199 on March 18, £400 on May 20, £770 on June 3, and £950 on June 29. Easy money! Stock prices were increasing so quickly that some said you could buy South Sea stock as you entered Garraway's Coffee House and sell it for a profit on the way out.

When people are eager to buy, swindlers are eager to sell. One company said that it was formed "for carrying on an undertaking of great advantage, but nobody is to know what it is." The company priced its shares at £100 each and promised an annual return of £100. The promotor sold all the shares in less than five hours, left England, and never returned. Another company described its business as "nitvender" or the selling of nothing. Yet, nitwits bought nitvender stock.

When the bubble popped, prices deflated as quickly as they had inflated. From its high of £950 in June, South Sea's stock price dropped to £400 on September 19 and £180 on September 28. By December, the price was back to where it had been before the madness began, down almost 90 percent from its peak.

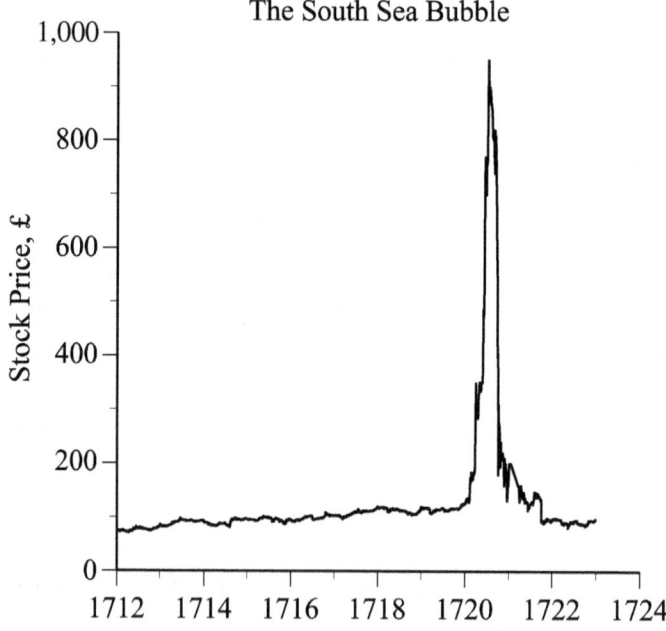

Lisa listened in amazement, but she had also been mulling over Jasmine's argument that value investors shun Beanie Babies and other collectibles. She blurted out,

What about gold? It doesn't produce any income.

Jasmine answered immediately:

Exactly. Value investors stay away from gold, despite its long-standing and near-universal appeal—for exactly the reason you gave: it doesn't generate any income. In fact, if you own gold, you may have to pay money to insure it and store it safely.

Jasmine then said that, back in 2012, Warren Buffett thought up a clever way of showing that gold is a crummy investment. He estimated that, if all the mined gold in the world were melded together, it would make a cube that was about 68 feet on each side and would easily fit inside a 90-foot-by-90-foot baseball diamond. At the market price at that time ($1,750 per ounce), this golden cube would be worth $9.6 trillion. Alternatively, one could use the $9.6 trillion to buy all U.S. cropland (400 million acres, generating $200 billion in annual income), 16 Exxon Mobils (each earning more than $40 billion annually), and still have $1 trillion left over (enough to buy two Apple computer companies in 2012). You could not, of course, literally buy 16 Exxons and 2 Apples; Buffett's point was that you could invest in a LOT of very profitable cropland and companies.

How would these two alternative investments fare over time? Buffett wryly observed that,

A century from now, the 400 million acres of farmland will have produced staggering amounts of corn, wheat, cotton, and other crops —and will continue to produce that valuable bounty, whatever the currency may be. Exxon Mobil will probably have delivered trillions of dollars in dividends to its owners and will also hold assets worth many more trillions (and, remember, you get 16 Exxons). The 170,000 tons of gold will be unchanged in size and still incapable of producing anything.

You can fondle the cube, but it will not respond.

Lisa said,

That's a great explanation. It makes sense and I will remember it always.

Jasmine said that this is why she shared it. She then added that there are other so-called investments besides gold that people are attracted to because others made money buying and then selling them. Vacant land is a good example:

The problem is that, as long as the land stays vacant, it isn't generating any income. In fact, the owner is losing money by paying property taxes and maybe also paying for maintenance, security, and insurance. True, some people have made fortunes buying vacant land that eventually was developed (think the Irvine Ranch), but there is a lot of undeveloped land in the United States that is just a money pit for its owners. When the total area of the United States is divided into 11 million census blocks, 44 percent of the blocks (containing 47% of the total area of the country), are completely vacant.

They are vacant for a reason. Nobody wants to develop them. Some will eventually be developed but most won't.

She then concluded with an unusually stern warning:

Stay away from collectibles, precious metals, and anything else that doesn't yield income. And don't get me started on bitcoin and other cryptocurrencies—otherwise known as digital tulip bulbs.

CHAPTER 29

A Benevolent Casino

Lisa telephoned Jasmine a few days before their next meeting and said that she was ready to talk stocks:

I've been dreading this conversation because I don't understand stocks and I'm afraid that I might do something really stupid. But now I'm ready to be a big girl and confront my fears—and I hope that you are going to convince me that I shouldn't be afraid.

Jasmine answered quickly and simply:

Hooray for you! Yep, I'm going to tell you why you shouldn't be afraid of stocks. In fact, you should embrace stocks. They can be a terrific investment if you follow a few sensible rules. More Tuesday.

They hung up, both looking forward to their next meeting.

Tuesday came and Lisa knocked on Jasmine's front door a few minutes early as usual, eager to get started.

Jasmine first explained what stocks are. When companies start out, the founders might use their own money, money from friends, or money from investors to get things going—to buy any equipment they need, maybe rent an office, pay employees, and cover any other expenses needed to get the business up and running:

Suppose you want to open a restaurant because you're a great cook and love cooking. (Just pretend, okay.) You will need to rent a place for your restaurant and either buy or rent an oven, refrigerator, dining tables and chairs, and everything else needed in your kitchen and in the serving area. Unless you and your friends are going to do it yourselves, you will need to hire a hostess, servers, and people to help in the kitchen. You will need to buy all the ingredients. You will probably need a lawyer, an accountant, and some way of publicizing your restaurant.

All these expenses add up. Even though the food may be great, about 60 percent of all restaurants fail in the first year and 80 percent in the first five years. Let's say you make it. In fact, you more than make it. There are lines outside, waiting to get in. People are making reservations weeks in advance and traveling long distances to eat at your restaurant.

Lisa said, "Great! If we are going to dream, we should make it a good dream." Jasmine nodded and said,

You decide to open more restaurants but you need more money, a lot more money, so you have an initial public offering (IPO) where you raise money by selling stock. The investors who buy stock in your restaurant are now part-owners of your soon-to-be-growing restaurant empire. With the help of a well-compensated investment bank, you might issue 1,000,000 shares of stock—keeping 600,000 shares for yourself and selling 400,000 shares at $40 apiece.

Lisa said, "So far, so good," and Jasmine continued:

Now, notice what just happened:

One, you raised $16 million (before banker fees), which should be enough to start expanding your business. Two, the 600,000 shares you kept for yourself are worth $24 million, which makes you a member of the millionaire's club. Three, since you own 60 percent of the stock, you still have voting control of the company.

Lisa said, "Sounds great! Where do I sign up?" Jasmine laughed,

Well, first, you need to learn how to make food that people will line up for!

Seriously, I'm getting to the point now. We're just assuming that you are a great cook.

Your restaurants are thriving, but you may not want to hold all 600,000 of your shares forever. Maybe you want to cash some of them in and buy a new house or maybe you want to invest some of your money elsewhere so that you don't have all your eggs in one basket. There are too many stories of entrepreneurs who were initially successful but, then lost everything when their company crashed and burned.

Also, some of your initial investors may want to sell some of their shares in order to buy a car or take a vacation or whatever. They bought stock in your company because they believed in you, and maybe they still do, but they were hoping to make some profits they could use to buy stuff—and now they want to do just that.

Fortunately, there are stock exchanges where people can sell shares of stock to other people. The most well-known is the New York Stock Exchange, but there are other exchanges too.

The point is that when you buy stock on the New York Stock Exchange, NASDAQ, or some other exchange, you are buying stock from other investors and becoming a part-owner of a company. When the company makes a profit and uses some of those profit to pay dividends to shareholders, you will get your share of the dividends. If you own 1 percent of the stock, you get 1 percent of the dividends.

Lisa said,

I thought the way you made money in the stock market was to buy some random stock before the price went up. If the price goes down, you lose money. It's like gambling in Vegas—you win sometimes and you lose most times—unless you're an insider who knows which stock prices are about to go up and which are about to go down.

Jasmine laughed,

There's a lot to unpack there. Let's talk through it one step at a time. First, you do make a profit (called a "capital gain") if the price of a stock you own goes up. But you can also make a profit if the stock price doesn't go up or even if the price goes down (a little). Remember, you are getting dividends too. If you buy a stock for $20 a share and it pays a $1 annual dividend, that's a 5 percent return, even if the price stays at $20.

In addition, most companies grow over time along with the overall economy. They make more profits and pay more dividends, so your initial $1 dividend might become $1.05 next year and $1.10 the year after. If the dividends keep growing, the stock price will probably increase, too, because, at some point, those growing dividends are irresistible at $20 a share.

Lisa said,

Okay, but who decides whether the stock price will go up or down?

Jasmine laughed again,

You do!

Well, not literally you all by yourself, but investors as a whole. Stock prices are determined by the prices buyers are willing to pay and the prices sellers are willing to accept. During every moment that the exchanges are open, the number of shares that people want to buy at the current market price is equal to the number of shares that people want to sell—the demand is equal to the supply.

If there is an increase in the demand for shares (perhaps because of good news about the company), the price will go up in order to persuade more people to sell shares to meet this increase in demand. If there is an increase in the supply of shares (more people wanting to sell), the price will fall in order to persuade more people to buy shares.

Lisa said,

You sound like one of those boring economics textbooks I had to read in college. Blah, blah, blah. That's not really how it works, is it? Can't the Wall Street insiders set prices wherever they want?

Jasmine laughed yet again,

Well, there was a time when scoundrels used a variety of dodgy schemes to manipulate stock prices and take advantage of the gullible and greedy.

For example, when a company was about to announce good or bad news, the top executives or other insiders who knew about the announcement ahead of time might buy or sell the company's stock before the announcement.

There were also pump-and-dump schemes where scammers would circulate phony good-news stories about a company and trade stock among themselves at ever higher prices, trying to lure in Greater Fools. After the price had been pumped up, the scammers would dump the stock by selling to fools at the artificially inflated prices.

Lisa said,

I knew it!

Jasmine was serious now:

As I said, those kinds of shenanigans were pretty common a long time ago, but now there are laws against insider trading and market manipulation and a government agency called the SEC enforces them the best they can.

There is still some manipulation and insider trading, but we can protect ourselves by: (1) only buying and selling companies like Apple, where tens of millions of shares are traded every day; and (2) not buying or selling just because the price is going up or down or because we read a dodgy news story. Instead, think about whether the price is reasonable relative to the company's earnings and dividends.

Even safer, buy an index fund such as Vanguard's S&P 500 index fund that contains hundreds of stocks. The effects of insider trading and pump-and-dump schemes on index funds is minimal.

When Lisa nodded yes, Jasmine went on:

We'll talk more about buying stocks next week. What I want to convince you of today is that the stock market is very different from gambling casinos in Las Vegas and elsewhere. In gambling casinos, the average better loses money in the long run. That's how the casinos can pay for the glitter and the all-you-can-eat buffets and still make a profit for the owners.

The stock market, on the other hand, can be thought of as a benevolent casino. It's like a casino in that there are seemingly unpredictable ups and downs in stock prices that give investors profits and losses—just like a slot machine or roulette wheel. On the other hand, the average stock investor makes money in the long run because stocks pay dividends and stock prices go up over time along with the economy, corporate profits, and dividends. There have been days, months, and even years when stock prices have fallen but, over the past one hundred years, the average annual return on stocks has been more than 10 percent. In Las Vegas, the odds favor the house. On Wall Street, the odds favor investors.

Okay. Tell me honestly: Did I convince you that the stock market is better than Las Vegas, that it is a benevolent casino?

Lisa grinned:

I'm convinced. I can't wait until next week.

CHAPTER 30

Stocks in the Long Run

Lisa showed up the next Tuesday, early as usual and eager to learn:

Hi! I can't believe how excited I am to learn about stocks. I've never bought a single share of stock and, before we talked last week, I thought I never would.

Jasmine replied,

Terrific! I'm not saying that stocks are a sure thing but I do think everyone should consider buying stocks and, certainly, no one should ever be afraid of them.

Jasmine explained that speculators who buy things such as Beanie Babies or Bitcoin because they hope to sell them to bigger fools at higher prices are at the mercy of the market. If the price goes down instead of up, they have nothing but an expensive lesson about the pitfalls of speculation.

Value investors are different. They view stocks, real estate, and other attractive investments as money machines that generate dividends, rent, and other income. If the price goes down, they still have the income from their investment. In fact, if the income is stable and the price drops, they may celebrate that they can buy more at a bargain price: "Wall Street is having a sale!"

Jasmine then showed Lisa two graphs. The first graph compared the dividends from the stocks in the S&P 500 with the prices of these stocks.

After Lisa had looked at the figure for a bit, Jasmine said

I want to point out several things. First stock prices are more volatile than dividends. They have a lot more short-term ups and downs because lots of investors overreact to news stories. Fear and greed are powerful emotions. Second, in the long run, dividends go up along with the U.S. economy and so do stock prices. Even though stock prices might drop substantially for a few days, weeks, months, or even years, they will eventually rebound and rise along with dividends. If stock prices stayed depressed while dividends doubled, tripled, quadrupled, stocks would be irresistibly cheap.

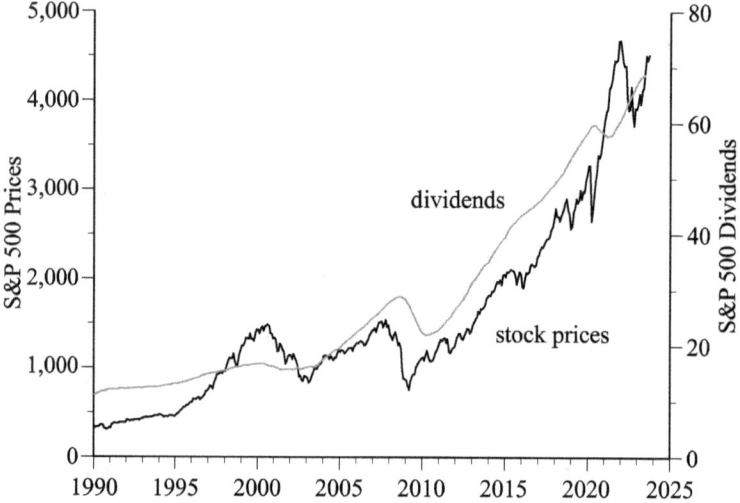

Jasmine then explained that, since dividends are paid out of earnings, stock prices in the long run should grow with corporate earnings. The second figure confirmed this.

Jasmine again let Lisa look at the figure for a while and then said,

This is very similar to the dividend graph because, after all, dividends are paid out of earnings. Corporate earnings are more volatile than dividends because they go up and down with the economy and companies try to keep their dividends on a smooth path but you can again see that, in the long run, earnings grow with the economy and so do stock prices.

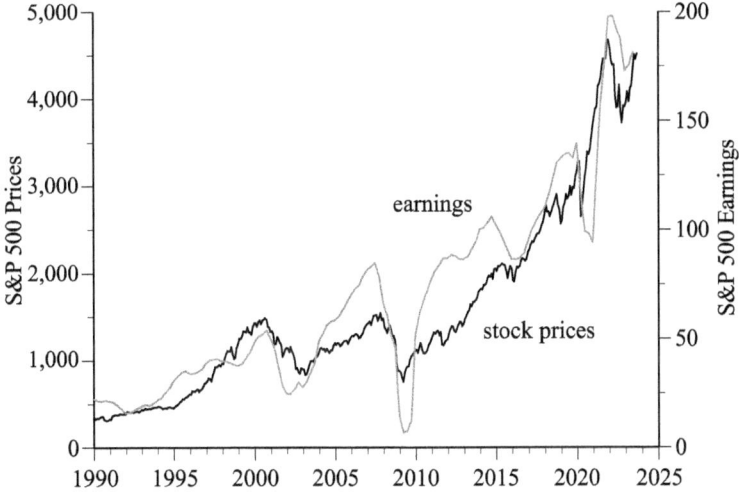

Jasmine held up the two graphs, one in each hand, and compared them. It was indeed striking how similar they were and how they both told the same story: stock prices zig and zag in the short run but ultimately go up with the economy. Jasmine said that, since 1990, the period shown in these two figures, the average annual return from owning the stocks in the S&P 500, including both dividends and capital gains, has been 10.2 percent.

> *Now let's look at a third graph. I promise this is the last one—but it may be more important than the first two.*
>
> *This graph shows what would have happened if you had invested $1 in the S&P 500, 30-year Treasury bonds, or 30-day Treasury bills back in 1990. The average annual returns were 10.2 percent for stocks, 5.7 percent for 30-year Treasury bonds, and 2.6 percent for 30-day Treasury bills. Do you remember the miracle of compound interest?*

Lisa said, "Of course," and Jasmine went on:

> *These seemingly modest differences in the annual returns from stocks, bonds, and bills result in huge differences in wealth after 30+ years. A $1 investment in stocks would have grown to more than $22 while an investments in Treasury bonds would have grown to a bit*

less than $6 and Treasury bills would have grown to a bit more than $2. A dollar kept in a safe deposit box or hidden under a mattress would still be just a dollar. This is why I have been so keen to cure your fear of the stock market.

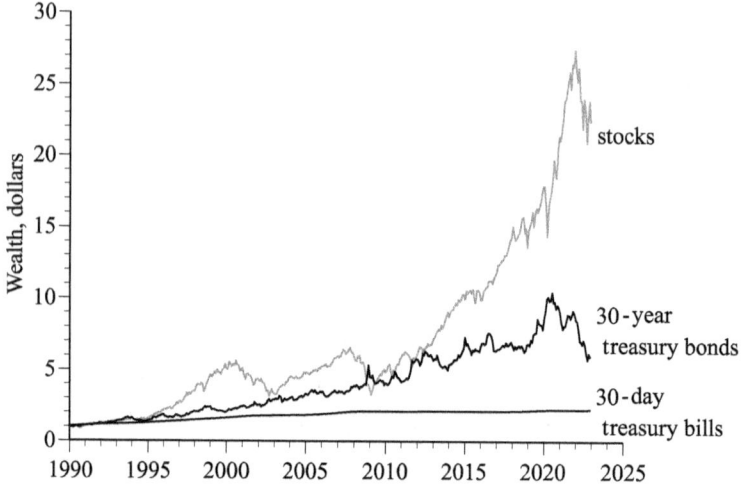

Lisa shook her head and said, "Wow! What a difference." She regretted not having invested in stocks in the past but was determined to invest in stocks in the future.

Then Jasmine said,

I have to warn you, stock prices do go up and down. They should be thought of as a long-term investment, not short-term speculation. Suppose, for example, that a young family has saved money for making a down payment on a house and the closing is in two weeks. They shouldn't get greedy and make a two-week plunge in the stock market. Similarly, an elderly couple living on their Social Security income shouldn't day-trade stocks with their monthly Social Security checks.

On the other hand, short-term fears can be unwarranted and expensive myopia. One of my clients came to me a few years ago, after she had just retired at age 62. She had saved nearly $800,000, all tucked into bank accounts. When I suggested that she venture outside of bank accounts, she told me, "I like you and I trust you, but it's important for you to understand that I don't want to lose the nest egg that I've built up over the past 40 years."

Lisa, said,

I can understand that. I wouldn't want my parents to lose what little they've saved. So, what did you tell her?

Jasmine replied.

I had three thoughts.

First, her nest egg would have been a lot larger—in fact, she would have had nearly $5 million—if she hadn't invested so conservatively for 40 years. She didn't need the money she was saving until she was in her 60s, so she shouldn't have spent 40 years worrying about short-term ups and downs in her investment returns.

Second, she owns a house with no mortgage and has pretty good monthly Social Security and pension income. In fact, she is saving some of her income and adding to her nest egg every month! Her nest egg is a good backup plan but she won't need it anytime soon for her day-to-day living expenses. Her Social Security benefits are indexed for inflation but her pension isn't, so there will probably come a time when she has to dip into her nest egg. In the meantime, she can try to grow her nest egg. If it goes down for a few months or years, it won't be a big deal. It will be a big deal if when she is, say, 82, her nest egg is a fifth of what it could have been. There may be short-term risks from investing aggressively, but there can be even larger long-term risks from investing conservatively.

My third thought was that her previous adviser hadn't done her any favors. It is easier to follow a CYA (cover-your-ass) strategy than to try to educate clients and risk being criticized or sued if something goes wrong. The great British economist, John Maynard Keynes, once wrote that, "Worldly wisdom teaches that it is better for reputation to fail conventionally than to succeed unconventionally." Keynes was a spectacularly successful investor because he dared to do what others were afraid to do.

> *Too many financial advisers think, "If my clients want to keep their money in checking accounts, earning little or no interest, I can protect my reputation by letting them do this. People always notice the stability and they seldom think about the money they could have made by doing something else. If a client does notice, I just say, 'That's what you wanted!'"*
>
> *I don't respect financial advisers who care more about themselves than about their clients.*

Lisa said, "I know that for sure and I really appreciate how honest and helpful you have been." Jasmine then said,

> *Thank you. I want you (and all my clients) to recognize that the key to successful investing is to ignore the short-term wiggles and jiggles in prices and think about the long-term payoff.*

Jasmine then said that even supposedly sophisticated investors can be distracted by short-term stock-price zigs and zags that they should ignore. She had gone to a wedding a few years ago and been seated next to "Amy," the president of a very wealthy private college. They hit it off and, soon, Amy was telling her that she was wrestling with a budget squeeze even though the college's tuition and fees were $80,000 a year and the college had an endowment at the time of roughly $2 million per student. The college's endowment spending rule allows it to spend 5 percent of the average value of the endowment over the previous five years, and 5 percent of $2 million is $100,000 per year per student.

Jasmine told Amy that the college seemed to have an embarrassment of riches. Amy agreed but said that the president before her had followed the cynical adage, "Spending expands to exhaust available income." That's a bad maxim for households and it is also a bad maxim for colleges. When Amy took over, she inherited a college that was overstaffed with hundreds of deans, associate deans, assistant deans, and assorted "support staff." She had little idea what most of them did every day. All she knew for certain was that everyone wanted pay increases to keep up with inflation and the college couldn't afford to do that.

Jasmine didn't have much to say to Amy about bloated bureaucracies except that she didn't want to work for one. She was curious, however, about how the endowment was invested. Amy said,

I don't know exactly. I do know that we pay some really smart people to make prudent investments. No bitcoin!

Amy said that she would find out more and get back to Jasmine. A few days later she called to say that the endowment managers used the widely followed 60–40 rule: 60 percent in stocks and 40 percent in bonds. The stock part is an S&P 500 index fund; the bond part is a Treasury-bond index fund:

The stocks give the endowment a good return and the bonds smooth out the day-to-day ups and downs.

Jasmine groaned,

I expected as much.
   The college is paying dearly for their (largely) unwarranted obsession with day-to-day ups and downs. The 5 percent withdrawal rule is based on the average value of the endowment over five years, not the value yesterday or two days ago. If the value of the endowment does sag for five years, the college's trustees can increase the withdrawal rate temporarily until the market recovers.

Amy said,

I have the returns over the past 10 years. They look pretty good: a 7.7 percent annual rate of return, which is well above the 5 percent withdrawal rule.

Jasmine said,

The results would have been even better if the college hadn't been paying the advisers for a CYA strategy that a simple computer program could do—60 percent in a stock index fund and 40 percent

in a bond index fund. More importantly, there is little reason to put 40 percent of the endowment in low-return bonds in order to smooth out the daily fluctuations in the endowment. Let me get back to you with some specific numbers.

She called back 20 minutes later:

A 100 percent investment in the S&P 500 over the past 10 years would have given the college an 11.9 percent annual rate of return. The value of the endowment today would be 47 percent higher than it actually is. If we go back to 1926, as far back as the data go, your endowment would be four times its current size if you had simply invested in a stock index fund instead of using 40 percent bonds to smooth out day-to-day fluctuations that you shouldn't care about.

Jasmine made her final pitch to Amy:

Your college is very wealthy and has a very long horizon—we hope, hundreds of years. It should invest accordingly. Yes, short-term fluctuations are a risk, but an even bigger risk is having a mediocre long-run performance.

After she finished telling this story to Lisa, she said:

The same is true of you if you think of how many decades you, your children, grandchildren, great grandchildren, and so on will live. Long-term growth is more important than short-term stability.

Lisa said, "I'm sold. Where do I start?" and Jasmine answered,

The simplest strategy is to invest in an index fund whenever you have money to invest. A more aggressive approach is to try to gauge whether stocks are cheap or expensive relative to dividends and earnings and then invest less when stocks seem expensive and more when they seem cheap. Another aggressive strategy is to pick a dozen or so individual stocks instead of buying hundreds of stocks in an index fund.

For now, until you gain more experience and confidence, I think your best strategy is to buy an index fund, preferably one with very low expenses.

Lisa said she was ready and they opened a Vanguard account right then and there.

CHAPTER 31

Mellowing Michael

Lisa telephoned Jasmine with news that absolutely could not wait until Tuesday. Her brother, Michael, had just stopped by her house for a surprise visit—and that was a huge surprise. Michael seldom called and he never came to Lisa's house. About the only time they saw each other was at family gatherings such as the Moon Festival, Christmas, and Chinese New Year.

It turns out that Michael had come by to say that he had embraced Jasmine's advice. He said that he had always known that he was the smartest realtor around, with an encyclopedic knowledge of the Irvine/Newport/Laguna housing market and he had the brains to put that vast knowledge to good use. He certainly had made enough money to prove that he was the best.

Michael was not easily satisfied. He wanted more. He may have needed more in order to soothe his insecurities. He may have wanted more in order to pamper his constantly revolving merry-go-round of girlfriends.

Either way, the daunting problem was that, to expand his empire, he would have to invade other real estate markets, such as Tustin, Huntington Beach, and Mission Viejo. True, Michael didn't know much about these markets, but he was confident that he could learn quickly. The bigger problem was that he would either have to spend precious hours driving longer distances or, else, hire assistants who would not only cost him money, but surely not be as good at closing deals.

Then he had an Aha! moment. His morning coffee meetings with Jasmine had revealed a better way to satisfy his ambitions. Smart businesses use the knowledge and insights they gain in making and selling one product to expand into other products. Look at how Apple grew from desktop computers to laptops, tablets, smartphones, watches, and more. Michael could use his mastery of the Irvine-area real estate market to buy dozens of rental properties and, as Jasmine explained, borrow money from banks relatively inexpensively and reap the rewards of leverage. It was like having a magical ATM. You put in a little and take out a lot.

He started cautiously and, once he saw how well it worked, he bought house after house. Soon he was making more money from his rental properties than he was making from his brokerage commissions. He even thought about quitting his realty business and focusing on his rental business, but then he realized that the real value of his brokerage business was not the commissions but the knowledge it gave him of the market and the opportunities it gave him to swoop in and buy well-priced properties before others could. He kept the realty business as a sideline, but it was a crucial sideline.

In any case, Michael had stopped by to say how much he appreciated Lisa! This was truly the first time in their lives that he had ever genuinely complimented or thanked her. And he was completely sincere. Jasmine had created the Aha! moment, but it was Lisa who had met Jasmine and was responsible for Michael meeting Jasmine.

Michael said that he knew all along that Jasmine and Lisa had been tag-teaming him about cryptocurrencies at the Harvest Moon dinner. At the time, he assumed that it was just some sort of sibling competition and he had shrugged it off because that wasn't the time or place for fireworks.

He now knew that it wasn't a contest at all. Lisa and Jasmine were not trying to embarrass him or score points. They were truly trying to be helpful. And they were, far beyond what any of them expected.

Michael hadn't turned into a marshmallow by any means, but he was definitely less intense and more mellow. He was willing to admit that he could learn from others and he was self-confident enough to say out loud that he was grateful for their help.

He proposed having regular Sunday dinners with Lisa, their parents, and other relatives who wanted to join in. He even suggested that they have the dinners at his Laguna Beach house and said that he would arrange for catering.

Lisa knew that the invitation to his home was just a gesture. They both knew that their mom would be thrilled with Sunday family dinners, but that she would definitely want to prepare the meal herself. Still, it was a nice gesture by Michael, and Lisa was very happy and optimistic about starting a Sunday dinner tradition that would bring the family together.

She laughed as she told Jasmine:

As Humphrey Bogart said in the last line in the movie Casablanca, "I think this is the beginning of a beautiful friendship."

I am so happy that Michael is mellowing and that we are becoming closer—and it is all because of you.

Then Jasmine spoke up:

I'm happy for you both, and happy you told me. A few days ago, UPS dropped off an enormous fruit basket from Oregon full of pears, apples, and other fruits that grow better in Oregon than in Irvine. The note said that it was from Michael and that I could expect boysenberries, marionberries, and Rainier cherries next year.

I don't think he is a man of few words, but the only other thing the note said was, "Thank you for everything!"

I was hoping this wasn't some kind of pickup ploy but I was afraid to ask, so I haven't said anything to him or anyone else, until now.

Lisa laughed,

You're safe! He likes his women younger, blonder, and dumber than you are.

My read of the situation is that Michael really is grateful for the terrific advice you gave him, but doesn't know how to come out and say it since he doesn't know you all that well—beyond you being smarter than anyone he has ever met.

Jasmine laughed, too:

Thank you for the kind words, but you're much too generous. You're both as smart as me, just in different ways. I know a lot of finance stuff because I've been thinking about finance stuff for a lot longer than you have, but you've learned really quickly. The truth is that the only things I know better than you do are quirky little nuggets that hardly ever come up. You now know enough to make good decisions well over 90 percent of the time. And as you make more decisions, your mastery will get even stronger.

Lisa smiled and said:

And thank you for your kind words. This has been a great day!

CHAPTER 32

A Life Reboot

As Lisa worked with Jasmine, she became increasingly satisfied—no, downright giddy—with her life. She was no longer depressed. She was no longer tired and grumpy during the day and restless at night. She was no longer burnt out. Part of the reason for her rejuvenation was that she had a job she loved but, perhaps more importantly, she made time for herself.

She did 30 minutes of yoga every morning, guided by YouTube videos. She played Mahjong every Thursday night with her parents and Uncle Andrew, not for money, but just for fun—and it was tremendous fun.

She joined a book club that met once a month. They drank wine, shared stories, and laughed. Sometimes they even talked about the books they were supposed to have read.

She was surprised to discover that she enjoyed cooking. Her meals became more than an efficient way of providing the fuel she needed to keep working. She learned that there is something deeply satisfying about assembling fresh ingredients, preparing a meal carefully, and then taking time to enjoy her creation. While she cooked or ate, her mind often frolicked through a seemingly endless array of fleeting thoughts—memories, anticipations, and more. Indeed, she sometimes had her most creative ideas when she was cooking or eating.

She often had a glass of cognac at night while she watched television, not to help her fall asleep but because she enjoyed it—especially if she nibbled aged cheese and dark chocolates while she sipped her cognac.

She got a dog to run with her when she went jogging and snuggle with her while she watched television. She chose a hypoallergenic goldendoodle, which is half poodle (smart) and half golden retriever (loving) and named her Peanut Butter, or Peanut for short—which was a joke since Peanut was a rambunctious 65 pounds. Lisa sometimes thought she should rename her Tigger—the Winnie-the-Pooh bundle of energy.

She even tried a double-double, animal style, from In-N-Out, a beloved Southern California hamburger chain headquartered in Irvine. A double-double is double-burger and double-cheese. Unlike other chains that precook burgers and put them under warmers to speed up service, the friendly workers at In-N-Out cook your burger *after* you order it and can customize your order in many ways, like making it "animal style" by cooking the burger smeared with mustard on both sides and topped with pickles, onions, cheese, and a special sauce.

You can also get a burger that is 3-by-3 or 4-by-4 (triple or quadruple meat and cheese), protein style (lettuce wrap), wish burger ("I wish this burger had meat"), or Flying Dutchman (nothing but two meat patties with two slices of cheese in between). Lisa had been skeptical, but had to admit that her double-double, animal style, tasted great. It was her first double-double but it would not be her last.

At the other end of the cheap-thrills price spectrum, she bought a 2004 vintage Colnago C50 road bike with Campagnolo components and, after several weeks of riding solo, she joined a cycling club. Irvine has more than 100 miles of protected off-street bike trails and nearly 300 miles of on-street bike lanes so the club had plenty of places to explore on their Sunday morning rides—what they called their Sunday "church of biking."

She met a terrific biking buddy in the cycling club, 20 years younger than her and as much in love with life as she now was. Lisa wasn't ready for marriage by any means, but she was ready for love.

Lisa also started a small vegetable garden in her backyard and wondered if she was turning into Jasmine. If so, that was a good thing! It had taken a while to sink in, but she now recognized the most important lesson she had learned from Jasmine. It wasn't the time value of money.

Lisa knew that she was very, very far from perfect and that, even so, Jasmine never judged her, never criticized her, never talked down to her. She accepted Lisa for who she was, with many good qualities and many annoying faults. Jasmine didn't explicitly try to change Lisa. She tried to help her make better financial decisions and she tried, by example, to show her a better way to live.

Lisa didn't need to work so hard at a job she didn't like. She didn't need to earn so much money or to spend so much money. She could take time to appreciate where she lived and how she lived. She could dance like no one was watching, sing like no one was listening.

Once Lisa understood this, she realized that it could be the same with her and her children (and maybe even with Erik). It wasn't Lisa's place to judge them. They had to find their own way, not be dragged reluctantly and resentfully, down paths that their mom chose for them.

She didn't have to improve her children and, anyway, she wasn't going to improve them by criticizing them. It was better to set a good example, the way Jasmine had set a good example for her. She was ready to do so.

One Sunday, after an exhilarating bike ride, Lisa picked up her phone and started dialing.

CHAPTER 33

Summing Up

It was time for their final formal session. Lisa could, of course, still call Jasmine or drop by whenever she had questions or just wanted to talk but there was no longer a need to meet regularly. Jasmine had pretty much covered everything Lisa needed to know.

Jasmine said,

Financial decisions often seem overwhelming. Some people don't like thinking about money. Some can be paralyzed by uncertainty because no one wants to make an expensive mistake. It is sometimes hard to even know where to begin.

I'm really proud of you, Lisa, for sticking with it and I'm proud of myself for, I hope, helping you learn more about making good financial decisions.

Lisa interrupted briefly:

Oh, yes, you have been more helpful than you will ever know.

Lisa said,

You're welcome. Today, I want to give you a short written summary that you can take home with you.

The key to making rational financial choices is to recognize the following six key principles that can be applied to essentially all financial decisions.

She handed Lisa this list:

1. Think on the margin. The relevant question is not how good things are, but whether your decision will make things better or

worse. When we think on the margin, we are less susceptible to the sunk-cost fallacy, which is when we let our decisions be affected by things that happened in the past and cannot be changed.
2. It's all about the cash. It's not about labels; it's about the dollars. Don't be distracted by jargon: amortization, depreciation, and so on. Just consider the money coming in and the money going out.
3. Think about alternatives. An alternative to going to college is to take a job. An alternative to buying a house is to rent one. An alternative to paying cash for a car, household appliance, or anything really is to take out a loan and invest the cash, remembering the useful rule of thumb that a loan is financially profitable if the rate of return you earn on your investments is higher than the loan rate.
4. Take the time value of money into account. A dollar today is more valuable than a dollar tomorrow. If you just add up the dollars without paying attention to the timing, you will make a total-payments error.
5. Recognize the power of compounding. Compounding means that, every year, you not only earn a return on your original investment but also on the earnings that you have already made on this investment. This compounding causes wealth to grow faster than might be expected. The Rule of 72 tells us that the time needed to double the value of an investment is approximately equal to 72 divided by the percentage return from the investment; for example, an investment earning 10 percent will double in 7.2 years.
6. Take uncertainty into account. Few things are certain. Don't assume everything is. We can handle uncertainty by comparing the costs and benefits for various plausible scenarios; for example, when considering the purchase of solar panels, make different assumptions about how long the panels will last and how fast the price of electricity will increase.

After reading it over, Lisa thanked Jasmine:

You know, it really isn't all that difficult! I was one of those people who thought financial decisions were super-complicated and so I avoided them. That was a super-expensive mistake. They really are just common sense.

Jasmine smiled:

Yep. We are no longer student/teacher. Now, we are friends for life.

About the Authors

Gary Smith earned his PhD in Economics from Yale University and is currently the Fletcher Jones Professor of Economics at Pomona College. He has won two teaching awards and written (or coauthored) more than 100 academic articles and 17 books. His most recent book, coauthored with Margaret Smith, is *The Power of Modern Value Investing: Beyond Indexing, Algos, and Alpha*, Palgrave Macmillan, 2024.

Margaret Smith is a certified financial planner, a certified integral coach, and an accredited Enneagram professional. She earned a simultaneous BA/MA *Summa Cum Laude* in Economics from Yale University, earned a PhD in Business Economics from Harvard University, and was an Economics professor for a decade. Her book, *Money: From Fear to Love*, 2011, is the first to relate the nine distinct Enneagram personality types to money and is the basis for workshops given around the world.

Index

Accessory dwelling unit (ADU), 67–71, 73, 80
Adverse selection, 105
Annuities, 101–105
Asymmetric information, 105

Beanie Babies, 49–52
Benevolent casino, 159–164
Bitcoin, 49, 158, 165
Borrowing, 34–37
Buffett, Warren, 153–154, 157

ChatGPT, 113–115
Compounding, 53, 137, 184
Credit cards, 27–29
Crossover, 121–126
CYA (cover-your-ass), 169, 171

Defined-benefit plans, 92
Defined-contribution plans, 92

Fox, Michael J., 45–46

Greater Fool Theory, 153–158

Homebuying, 59–66
Homemade annuity, 102

Individual retirement account (IRA), 93–95
Investment, 22, 29–30, 50–62, 76, 83, 86–88, 94, 102, 154, 157–160, 167–169, 184
Irvine Company, 4

Kotlikoff, Laurence, 79–81, 83

Large language models (LLMs), 113–114, 116
Life insurance, 97–100

Mid-Autumn Festival (or Moon Festival), 49–54

Pump-and-dump schemes, 163–164

Recreational vehicles (RVs), 145–148
Rental properties, 55–58
Required minimum distributions (RMDs), 95
Retirement communities, 107–111
Retirement plans, 91–96
Rule of 72, 53–54, 184

Saving, 121–126
Social Security, 79–89
Solar panels, 73–76
South Sea Bubble, 155–156
Spending, 133–141
Sperling's Rule, 39–43
Stocks, 165–173

Time value of money, 31–38
Total payments error, 32–33
Tulip bulb bubble, 155

Uncertainty, 74, 183, 184
University of California, Irvine (UCI), 4, 18, 59

Vacation homes, 143–145
Veblen, Thorstein, 122

OTHER TITLES IN THE FINANCE AND FINANCIAL MANAGEMENT COLLECTION

Jeffrey Edwards, Old Dominion University, *Editor*

- *Wealth Management* by Erik Lie
- *Mastering Options* by Philip Cooper
- *The Corporate Executive's Guide to General Investing* by Paul Mladjenovic
- *The Human Factor in Mergers, Acquisitions, and Transformational Change* by Muhammad Rafique
- *Understanding Cryptocurrencies* by Ariel Santos-Alborna
- *Understanding the Financial Industry Through Linguistics* by Richard C. Robinson
- *Sustainable Finance and Impact Investing* by Alan S. Gutterman
- *The Non-Timing Trading System* by George O. Head
- *Small Business Finance and Valuation* by Rick Nason and Dan Nordqvist
- *Finance for Non-Finance Executives* by Anurag Singal
- *Blockchain Hurricane* by Kate Baucherel
- *Risk Management for Nonprofit Organizations* by Rick Nason and Omer Livvarcin
- *Conservative Options Trading* by Michael C. Thomsett

Concise and Applied Business Books

The Collection listed above is one of 30 business subject collections that Business Expert Press has grown to make BEP a premiere publisher of print and digital books. Our concise and applied books are for…

- Professionals and Practitioners
- Faculty who adopt our books for courses
- Librarians who know that BEP's Digital Libraries are a unique way to offer students ebooks to download, not restricted with any digital rights management
- Executive Training Course Leaders
- Business Seminar Organizers

Business Expert Press books are for anyone who needs to dig deeper on business ideas, goals, and solutions to everyday problems. Whether one print book, one ebook, or buying a digital library of 110 ebooks, we remain the affordable and smart way to be business smart. For more information, please visit www.businessexpertpress.com, or contact sales@businessexpertpress.com.

www.ingramcontent.com/pod-product-compliance
Lightning Source LLC
Chambersburg PA
CBHW070402240426
43661CB00056B/2499